Yarn

AUNT LYDIA'S *Classic Crochet Thread,*
Size 10, each ball approx 350yd/320m (cotton)
• 1 ball #450 Aqua (A)
AUNT LYDIA'S *Fashion Crochet Thread,* Size 3,
each ball approx 150yd/137m (cotton)
• 1 ball #0065 Teal (B)

Crochet hook

Size 6 (1.8mm) steel crochet hook for size 10
thread *or size to obtain gauge*
Size 4 (2.0mm) steel crochet hook for size 3
thread *or size to obtain gauge*

Notions

Sewing needle with large eye

Showcase your special memories with these gorgeous crochet photo mats.

Stitch Glossary

sc2tog (sc 2 stitches together) [Insert hook into next st, yarn over, draw up a loop] twice, yarn over and draw through all 3 loops on hook

Finished Measurements

Frames can be made to fit any mat.

Gauge

Strip of Frame #1 = ¾"/2cm wide using Size 6 (1.8mm) hook and size 10 thread
Strip of Frame #2 = 1"/2.5cm wide using Size 4 (2.0mm) hook and size 3 thread
Remember to check gauge for best results!

How to Make a Gauge Swatch

Work several inches of Frame #1 or Frame #2 with specified thread and hook. With size 10 thread the width of the frame strip should be approx ¾"/2cm wide. With size 3 thread the width of the frame strip should be approx 1"/2.5cm wide.

Note

Frame strips are worked from corner to corner. Four strips are then sewn together at corners to form frame. For each frame, make 4 strips. For a 5 x 7"/12.5 x 18cm frame make two 5"/12.5cm and two 7"/18cm strips. For an 8 x 10"/20.5 x 25.5cm frame make two 8"/20.5cm and two 10"/25.5cm strips.

Frame #1 (make 4 strips)

With A and Size 6 (1.8mm) hook, ch 2.

Beginning Miter

Row 1 2 sc in 2nd ch from hook—2 sc.
Row 2 Ch 1, turn, 2 sc in first—sc, sc in next sc—3 sc.
Row 3 Ch 1, turn, sc in first 2 sc, 2 sc in last sc—4 sc.
Row 4 Ch 1, turn, 2 sc in first sc, sc in last 3 sc—5 sc.

Frame Strip

Row 1 Ch 3 (counts as first dc), turn, sk 1 st, dc in next st, ch 3, sk 2 sts, sl st in next sc.
Row 2 Ch 4 (counts as dc, ch 1), turn, [dc, ch 1] in ch–3 sp 7 times, dc in next dc, dc in top of turning ch—10 dc.
Row 3 Ch 3, turn, sk first dc, dc in next dc, ch 3, sk next ch–1 sp, sk next dc, sl st in next ch–1 sp; leave remaining sts unworked.
Repeat Rows 2 and 3 until piece measures ½"/1.5cm less than desired length (for example, if a 7"/18cm strip is desired, work until piece measures 6½"/16.5cm) ending with Row 2.

Ending Miter

Row 1 Ch 1, turn, sc in first 2 dc, sc in next ch–1 sp, sc in next dc, sc in next ch–1 sp; leave remaining sts unworked—5 sc.
Row 2 Ch 1, turn, sc2tog, sc in last 3 sc—4 sc.
Row 3 Ch 1, turn, sc in first 2 sc, sc2tog—3 sc.
Row 4 Ch 1, turn, sc2tog, sc in last sc—2 sc.
Row 5 Ch 1, turn, sc2tog—1 sc.
Fasten off.
Repeat to make 4 strips of desired lengths.

Finishing

Matching mitered edges of strips, lay out strips to form

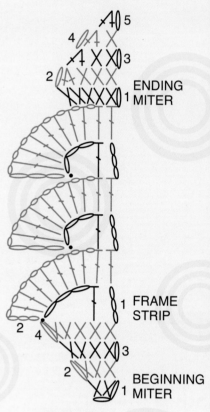

FRAME #1

frame. Sew corner edges together. Weave in all ends.

Frame #2 (make 4 strips)
With B and size 4 (2.0mm) hook, ch 2.

Beginning Miter
Row 1 2 sc in 2nd ch from hook—2 sc.
Row 2 Ch 1, turn, sc in first sc, 2 sc in last sc—3 sc.
Row 3 Ch 1, turn, 2 sc in first sc, sc in last 2 sc—4 sc.
Row 4 Ch 1, turn, sc in first 3 sc, 2 sc in last sc—5 sc.

Frame Strip
Row 1 Ch 4, turn, hdc in first st, ch 1, sk 1 st, hdc in next st, ch 1, sk 1 st, hdc in last st.
Row 2 Ch 2, turn, hdc in first hdc, [hdc in next ch–1 sp, hdc in next hdc] twice—5 hdc.
Repeat Rows 1 and 2 until piece measures ½"/1.5cm less than desired length (for example, if a 7"/18cm strip is desired, work until piece measures 6½"/16.5cm), ending with Row 2.

Ending Miter
Row 1 Ch 1, turn, sc in each hdc across—5 sc.
Row 2 Ch 1, turn, sc in first 3 sc, sc2tog—4 sc.
Row 3 Ch 1, turn, sc2tog, sc in last 2 sc—3 sc.
Row 4 Ch 1, turn, sc in first sc, sc2tog—2 sc.
Row 5 Ch 1, turn, sc2tog.
Fasten off.
Repeat to make 4 strips of desired lengths.

Finishing
Matching mitered edges of strips, lay out strips to form frame. Sew corner edges together. Weave in all ends.

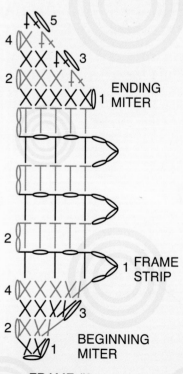

FRAME #2

let it snow Doily

Yarn
AUNT LYDIA'S *Bamboo Crochet Thread*,
Size 10, each ball approx 300yd/274m
(viscose from bamboo)
• 1 ball #226 Natural

Crochet hook
Size 7 (1.65mm) steel crochet hook *or
size to obtain gauge*

Notions
Yarn needle
9"/23cm square cloth photo album with
3½"/9cm square frame opening
4¼ x 4¾"/11 x 12cm cardstock
in solid color of choice (for
background of snowflake)

Get nostalgic with this sweet snowflake motif, just the right size for decorating an album of wintry memories.

Stitch Glossary
picot Ch 3, sl st in last sc made.
tr–picot (triple picot) Ch 3, (sl s t, ch 4, sl st, ch 3, sl st) in last sc made.

Finished Measurements
Snowflake measures approx 3¼"/8.5cm diameter between points.

Gauge
Rounds 1–3 = 2"/5cm diameter between points.
Remember to check gauge for best results!

Snowflake
Ch 5; join with sl st in first ch to form a ring.
Round 1 (RS) Ch 1, sc in ring, [ch 5, sc in ring] 5 times; join with ch 2, dc in first sc (counts as ch–5 sp)—6 ch–5 sps.
Round 2 Sc in first ch–5 sp (formed by ch 2, dc join), [ch 7, sc in next ch–5 sp] 5 times; join with ch 3, tr in first sc (counts as ch–7 sp)—6 ch–7 sps.
Round 3 (Sl st, ch 3 [counts as dc], 2 dc) in first ch–7 sp (formed by ch 3, tr join), *(3 dc, ch 5, 3 dc) in next ch–7 sp; repeat from * 4 more times, 3 dc in first ch–7 sp, ch 5; join with sl st in top of beg ch–3—36 dc and 6 ch–5 sps.
Round 4 Sl st in next 2 dc, sl st in sp before next 3–dc group, ch 3 (counts as hdc, ch 1), *(dc, ch 2, dc, ch 3, tr, ch 3, dc, ch 2, dc) in next ch–5 sp, ch 1, hdc in sp between

next two 3–dc groups, ch 1; repeat from * 4 more times, (dc, ch 2, dc, ch 3, tr, ch 3, dc, ch 2, dc) in next ch–5 sp, ch 1; join with sl st in 2nd ch of beg ch–3—6 tr, 24 dc and 6 hdc.
Round 5 Ch 1, sc in same ch as join, *picot, sk next ch–1 sp, sc in next dc, 2 sc in next ch–2 sp, sc in next dc, picot, 3 sc in next ch–3 sp, sc in next tr, tr–picot, 3 sc in next ch–3 sp, sc in next dc, picot, 2 sc in next ch–2 sp, sc in next dc, sk next ch–1 sp, sc in next hdc; repeat from * 4 more times, picot, sk next ch–1 sp, sc in next dc, 2 sc in next ch–2 sp, sc in next dc, picot, 3 sc in next ch–3 sp, sc in next tr, tr–picot, 3 sc in next ch–3 sp, sc in next dc, picot, 2 sc in next ch–2 sp, sc in next dc, sk next ch–1 sp; join with sl st in first sc—6 tr–picots and 18 picots. Fasten off.

Rose Callahan

Finishing

Weave in all ends. Wash and block snowflake.

Assembly

With right side facing, center snowflake onto cardstock. Remove the clear vinyl from front frame opening of photo album and line it up with the cardstock over top of snowflake. Carefully slide all three layers (cardstock, snowflake, vinyl) into frame opening. If needed, remove layers and adjust snowflake to center in opening.

Tip

These little snowflakes make great ornaments or gift decorations. Stitch them up in white and use spray starch to stiffen.

the art of Lace

Yarn
AUNT LYDIA'S *Fashion Crochet Thread*,
Size 3, approx 150yd/137m per ball (cotton)
• 2 balls #12 Black or
• 2 balls #201 White

Crochet hook
Size B/1 (2mm) crochet hook *or
size to obtain gauge*

Notions
20 x 20" foamcore
plastic wrap
20 x 20" stretched canvas
Acrylic Paint
Paintbrushes
Craft Glue
Rust–proof pins for blocking

From super small to supersized, a dainty doily from the past gets a modern–scale makeover. Why struggle with thread when you can work big—for colossally cool results?

Finished Measurements
Approx 21"/53.5cm in diameter.

Gauge
Rounds 1–4 = 4½"/11.5cm in diameter using size B/1 (2mm) crochet hook.
Remember to check gauge for best results!

How To Make A Gauge Swatch
Work Rounds 1–4 of Doily instructions (below). Resulting gauge swatch should measure approx 4½"/11.5cm in diameter. Adjust hook size if necessary to obtain correct gauge.

Note
The final (ch 2, dc) at the end of some rounds counts as a ch–5 sp.

Doily
Starting at center, ch 10.
Round 1 Tr in 10th ch from hook, (ch 5, tr in same ch) 6 times; join with ch 2, dc in 4th ch of beg ch–10 (counts as ch–5 sp)—8 ch–5 sp.
Round 2 4 dc in first ch–5 sp (formed by ch 2, dc), 7 sc in each ch–5 sp around, end with 3 sc in first ch–5 sp; join with sl st in first dc—56 sc.
Round 3 Ch 14 (counts as tr, ch 10), * sk 6 sc, tr in next sc, ch 10; repeat from * around, join with sl st in 4th ch of beg ch–14—8 ch–10 sp.
Round 4 Ch 1, *13 sc in next ch–10 sp, sc in next tr; repeat from * around; join with sl st in first sc—112 sc.
Round 5 Ch 1, sc in first 13 sc, *ch 5, sk 1 sc, sc in next 13 sc; repeat from * around; join with ch 2, dc in beg ch–1 (counts as ch–5 sp)—8 groups of 13 sc and 8 ch–5 sp.
Round 6 * Ch 5, sk 1 sc, sc in next 11 sc, ch 5, sk 1 sc, sc in next ch–5 sp; repeat from * around; ending last repetition with ch 2, dc in dc of Round 5—8 groups of 11 sc and 16 ch–5 sp.
Round 7 Ch 5, sc in next ch–5 sp, ch 5, sk 1 sc, sc in next 9 sc, sk 1 sc, * (ch 5, sc in next ch–5 sp) twice, ch 5, sk 1 sc, sc in next 9 sc, sk 1 sc; repeat from * around; join with ch 2, dc in dc of Round 6—8 groups of 9 sc and 24 ch–5 sp.
Rounds 8–11 Work as for Round 7 working 1 more ch–5 between groups of sc, and 2 fewer sc in each group of sc in each round—56 ch–5 sp.
Round 12 Turn, sl st in next ch–5 sp (made prior to ch–5 sp formed by ch 2, dc), ch 1, turn, sc in same ch–5 sp, *sc in next ch–5 sp, (ch 5, sc in next ch–5 sp) 6 times; repeat from * around, ending last repetition with ch 2, dc in first sc—48 ch–5 sp.
Round 13 * Ch 5, sc in next ch–5 sp; repeat from * around; join with ch 2, dc in dc of Round 12.
Round 14 * Ch 5, (tr, ch 5, tr) in next ch–5 sp, (ch 5, sc in next ch–5 sp) 5 times; repeat from * around, ending last repetition with ch 2, dc in dc of Round 13.
Round 15 * Ch 5, sk next ch–5 sp, 10 tr in next ch–5 sp, ch 5, sk next ch–5 sp, sc in next ch–5 sp, (ch 5, sc in next ch–5 sp) 3 times; repeat from * around, ending last repetition with ch 2, dc in dc of Round 14.
Round 16 * Ch 5, sk next ch–5 sp, (tr in next tr, ch 1) 9

FIRST PINEAPPLE

EDGING

times, tr in next tr, ch 5, sk next ch–5 sp, sc in next ch–5 sp, (ch 5, sc in next ch–5 sp) twice; repeat from * around, ending last repetition with ch 2, dc in dc of Round 15.

Round 17 * Ch 5, sk next ch–5 sp, (sc in next ch–1 sp, ch 3) 8 times, sc in next ch–1 sp, ch 5, sk next ch–5 sp, sc in next ch–5 sp, ch 5, sc in next ch–5 sp; repeat from * around, ending last repetition with ch 2, dc in dc of Round 16.

Round 18 Ch 1, sc in first ch–5 sp (formed by ch 2, dc), ch 7, sk next ch–5 sp, (sc in next ch–3 sp, ch 3) 7 times, sc in next ch–3 sp, ch 7, sk next ch–5 sp, * sc in next ch–5 sp, ch 7, sk next ch–5 sp, (sc in next ch–3 sp, ch 3) 7 times,

sc in next ch–3 sp, ch 7, sk next ch–5 sp; repeat from * around, join with sl st in first sc.

Round 19 Ch 11 (counts as tr, ch 7), sk next ch–7 sp, (sc in next ch–3 sp, ch 3) 6 times, sc in next ch–3 sp, ch 7, sk next ch–7 sp, * (tr, ch 5, tr) in next sc, ch 7, sk next ch–7 sp, (sc in next ch–3 sp, ch 3) 6 times, sc in next ch–3 sp, ch 7, sk next ch–7 sp; repeat from * around, tr in sc of Round 18, ch 2, dc in 4th ch of beg ch–11.

Round 20 Ch 11 (counts as tr, ch 7), sk next ch–7 sp, (sc in next ch–3 sp, ch 3) 5 times, sc in next ch–3 sp, ch 7, sk next ch–7 sp, * (tr, ch 5, tr, ch 5, tr) in next ch–5 sp, ch 7, sk next ch–7 sp, (sc in next ch–3 sp, ch 3) 5 times, sc in

next ch–3 sp, ch 7, sk next ch–7 sp; repeat from * around, (tr, ch 5, tr) in last ch–5 sp (formed by ch 2, dc); join with ch 2, dc in 4th ch of beg ch–11.

Round 21 Ch 9 (counts as tr, ch 5), tr in first ch–5 sp (formed by ch 2, dc), ch 5, * sk next ch–7 sp, (sc in next ch–3 sp, ch 3) 4 times, sc in next ch–3 sp, ch 5, sk next ch–7 sp, [(tr, ch 5, tr, ch 5, tr) in next ch–5 sp, ch 5] twice; repeat from * around, ending last repetition with (tr, ch 5) in last ch–5 sp (formed by ch 2, dc); join with sl st in 4th ch of beg ch–9. Now work pineapples individually as follows:

First Pineapple

Row 1 Sl st in first ch–5 sp (formed by beg ch–9), ch 9 (counts as tr, ch–5), tr in same ch–5 sp, ch 7, sk next ch–5 sp, (sc in next ch–3 sp, ch 3) 3 times, sc in next ch–3 sp, ch 7, sk next ch–5 sp, (tr, ch 5, tr) in next ch–5 sp.

Row 2 Ch 9 (counts as tr, ch 5), turn, tr in first ch–5 sp, ch 7, sk next ch–7 sp, (sc in next ch–3 sp, ch 3) twice, sc in next ch–3 sp, ch 7, sk next ch–7 sp, (tr, ch 5, tr) in next ch–5 sp.

Row 3 Ch 9, turn, tr in first ch–5 sp, ch 7, sk next ch–7 sp, sc in next ch–3 sp, ch 3, sc in next ch–3 sp, ch 7, sk next ch–7 sp, (tr, ch 5, tr) in next ch–5 sp.

Row 4 Ch 9, turn, tr in first ch–5 sp, ch 7, sk next ch–7 sp, sc in next ch–3 sp, ch 7, sk next ch–7 sp, tr in last ch–5 sp, ch 2, turn, sl st in top of 4th ch of beg ch–9, ch 2, turn, tr in last ch–5 sp. Fasten off.

Next Pineapple

Row 1 Sk 3 ch–5 sps of Round 21, join thread in next ch–5

sp, ch 9 (counts as tr, ch 5), tr in same ch–5 sp, ch 7, sk next ch–5 sp, (sc in next ch–3 sp, ch 3) 3 times, sc in next ch–3 sp, ch 7, sk next ch–5 sp, (tr, ch 5, tr) in next ch–5 sp.

Rows 2–4 Work as for first pineapple Rows 2–4. Fasten off. Complete remaining pineapples in the same manner.

Finishing

Edging

With right side facing, join thread with sl st in any space of edge.

Round 1 Ch 1, work 7 sc in each of the 2 sp on either side of each pineapple point, and work 5 sc in each of the other sp around; join with sl st in first sc. Fasten off. Weave in all ends.

Blocking and Mounting

Cover foamcore with plastic wrap.

Block Doily Moisten doily and pin to foamcore, stretching to correct size and shape; allow to dry.

Stiffen Doily Mix equal parts craft glue and water; brush this on right side of doily, soaking thoroughly. Let dry overnight.

Mount Doily Paint canvas your color of choice and allow to dry. When doily is dry, remove from foamcore. Brush craft glue on wrong side and adhere doily to painted canvas. Be sure to smooth and press doily firmly to ensure it attaches to the canvas. Let dry overnight.

sunburst Bowls

Yarn

J&P COATS *Royale Fashion Crochet*
Thread, size 3, each ball approx
150yd/137m (cotton)
- 1 ball #65 Warm Teal (A)
- 1 ball #486 Navy (B)
- 1 ball #226 Natural (C)
- 1 ball #6 Scarlett (D)
- 1 ball #423 Maize (E)
- 1 ball #325 Tangerine (F)

Crochet hook

Size 1 (2.75mm) steel crochet hook *or size to obtain
gauge*

Notions

Stitch marker
Yarn needle

Tapestry crochet creates brilliant sections of color in this stunning piece. Use it to corral jewelry, or simply display it on its own.

Stitch Glossary

sc2tog (sc 2 sts together) [Insert hook in next st, yo and draw up a lp] 2 times, yo and draw through all 3 lps on hook.

Finished Measurements

Approx 10"/25.5cm diameter x 1¼"/3cm high.

Gauge

Rounds 1–8 = 2¾"/7cm diameter
Remember to check gauge for best results!

How To Make A Gauge Swatch
Rounds 1–8 Work same as Rounds 1–8 on basket. Swatch should measure approx 2¾4"/7cm diameter. Adjust hook size if necessary to obtain correct gauge.

Notes

1 This project is worked in a spiral. To keep track of where each round ends, place stitch marker in top of last st of round. Remove stitch marker from last st and place it in new last st at end of each round.
2 Tapestry crochet is worked by carrying unused thread(s) over top 2 loops of sts in previous round while working sts over carried thread(s), encasing thread(s) inside sts.
3 To change colors, work st until 2 loops remain on hook; drop working thread, yarn over with next color thread and complete st. Carry old color with other carried threads.

Basket

With A, ch 4, leaving a 12"/30.5cm tail; join with sl st in first ch to form a ring.
Round 1 Work 6 sc in ring while carrying tail—6 sc.
Round 2 Carry A tail and start to carry B. With A, work 2 sc in each sc around—12 sc.
Round 3 Carry A tail and B and start to carry C. With A, work 2 sc in each sc around—24 sc.
Round 4 Carry A tail and B and C and start to carry D. With A, *sc in next sc, 2 sc in next sc; repeat from * 11 more times—36 sc.
Round 5 Carry A tail and B, C and D and start to carry E. With A, *sc in next 2 sc, 2 sc in next sc; repeat from * 11 more times—48 sc.
Round 6 Cut A tail, carry B, C, D and E and start to carry F. With A, *sc in next 3 sc, 2 sc in next sc; repeat from * 11 more times—60 sc.
Note Always carry 5 threads not in use throughout rest of basket.
Round 7 With A, *sc in next 4 sc, 2 sc in next sc; repeat from * 11 more times—72 sc.
Round 8 With A, *sc in next 5 sc, 2 sc in next sc; repeat from * 11 more times—84 sc.
Round 9 With B, *sc in next 6 sc, 2 sc in next sc; repeat from * 11 more times—96 sc.
Round 10 *Sc in next 7 sc with C, 2 sc in next sc with B; repeat from * 11 more times—108 sc.
Round 11 *Sc in next sc with B, sc in next 6 sc with C, sc in next sc with B, 2 sc in next sc with D; repeat from * 11 more times—120 sc.
Round 12 *Sc in next sc with D, sc in next sc with B, sc in next 5 sc with C, sc in next sc with B, sc in next sc with D, 2 sc in next sc with D; repeat from * 11 more times—132 sc.
Round 13 *Sc in next 2 sc with D, sc in next sc with B, sc in next 4 sc with C, sc in next sc with B, sc in next 2 sc with D, 2 sc in next sc with D; repeat from * 11 more times—144 sc.
Round 14 *Sc in next 3 sc with D, sc in next sc with B, sc in next 3 sc with C, sc in next sc with B, sc in next 3 sc with D, 2 sc in next sc with D; repeat from * 11 more times—156 sc.

Round 15 *Sc in next 4 sc with D, sc in next sc with B, sc in next 2 sc with C, sc in next sc with B, sc in next 4 sc with D, 2 sc in next sc with D; repeat from * 11 more times—168 sc.

Round 16 *Sc in next 5 sc with D, sc in next sc with B, sc in next sc with C, sc in next sc with B, sc in next 5 sc with D, 2 sc in next sc with D; repeat from * 11 more times—180 sc.

Round 17 *Sc in next 6 sc with D, sc in next 2 sc with B, sc in next 6 sc with D, 2 sc in next sc with D; repeat from * 11 more times—192 sc.

Round 18 *Sc in next 7 sc with D, sc in next sc with B, sc in next 7 sc with D, 2 sc in next sc with D; repeat from * 11 more times—204 sc.

Round 19 *Sc in next 7 sc with D, 2 sc in next sc with B, sc in next 9 sc with D; repeat from * 11 more times—216 sc.

Round 20 *Sc in next 7 sc with D, sc in next sc with B, 2 sc in next sc with E, sc in next sc with B, sc in next 15 sc with D, sc in next sc with B, 2 sc in next sc with F, sc in next sc with B, sc in next 8 sc with D; repeat from * 5 more times—228 sc.

Round 21 *Sc in next 7 sc with D, sc in next sc with B, sc in next sc with E, 2 sc in next sc with E, sc in next sc with E, sc in next sc with B, sc in next 14 sc with D, sc in next sc with B, sc in next sc with F, 2 sc in next sc with F, sc in next sc with F, sc in next sc with B, sc in next 7 sc with D; repeat from * 5 more times—240 sc.

Round 22 *Sc in next 7 sc with D, sc in next sc with B, sc in next 2 sc with E, 2 sc in next sc with E, sc in next 2 sc with E, sc in next sc with B, sc in next 13 sc with D, sc in next sc with B, sc in next 2 sc with F, 2 sc in next sc with F, sc in next 2 sc with F, sc in next sc with B, sc in next 6 sc with D; repeat from * 5 more times—252 sc.

Round 23 *Sc in next 7 sc with D, sc in next sc with B, sc in next 3 sc with E, 2 sc in next sc with E, sc in next 3 sc with E, sc in next sc with B, sc in next 12 sc with D, sc in next sc with B, sc in next 3 sc with F, 2 sc in next sc with F, sc in next 3 sc with F, sc in next sc with B, sc in next 5 sc with D; repeat from * 5 more times—264 sc.

Round 24 *Sc in next 7 sc with D, sc in next sc with B, sc in next 4 sc with E, 2 sc in next sc with E, sc in next 4 sc with E, sc in next sc with B, sc in next 11 sc with D, sc in next sc with B, sc in next 4 sc with F, 2 sc in next sc with F, sc in next 4 sc with F, sc in next sc with B, sc in next 4 sc with D; repeat from * 5 more times—276 sc.

Round 25 *Sc in next 7 sc with D, sc in next sc with B, sc in next 5 sc with E, 2 sc in next sc with E, sc in next 5 sc with E, sc in next sc with B, sc in next 10 sc with D, sc in next sc with B, sc in next 5 sc with F, 2 sc in next sc with F, sc in next 5 sc with F, sc in next sc with B, sc in next 3 sc with D; repeat from * 5 more times—288 sc.

Round 26 *Sc in next sc with D, sc2tog with D, sc in next 4 sc with D, sc in next sc with B, sc in next 6 sc with E, 2 sc in next sc with E, sc in next 6 sc with E, sc in next sc with B, sc in next 3 sc with D, sc2tog with D, sc in next 4 sc with D, sc in next sc with B, sc in next 6 sc with F, 2 sc in next sc with F, sc in next 6 sc with F, sc in next sc with B, sc in next 2 sc with D; repeat from * 5 more times.

Round 27 *Sc in next sc with D, sc2tog with D, sc in next 3 sc with D, sc in next sc with B, sc in next 7 sc with E, 2 sc in next sc with E, sc in next 7 sc with E, sc in next sc with B, sc in next 2 sc with D, sc2tog with D, sc in next 3 sc with D, sc in next sc with B, sc in next 7 sc with F, 2 sc in next sc with F, sc in next 7 sc with F, sc in next sc with B, sc in next sc with D; repeat from * 5 more times.

Round 28 *Sc in next sc with D, sc2tog with D, sc in next 2 sc with D, sc in next sc with B, sc in next 8 sc with E, 2 sc in next sc with E, sc in next 8 sc with E, sc in next sc with B, sc in next sc with D, sc2tog with D, sc in next 2 sc with D, sc in next sc with B, sc in next 8 sc with F, 2 sc in next sc with F, sc in next 8 sc with F, sc in next sc with B; repeat from * 5 more times; sc in first sc with D—289 sc.

Round 29 *Sc2tog with D, sc in next sc with D, sc in next sc with B, sc in next 9 sc with E, 2 sc in next sc with E, sc in next 9 sc with E, sc in next sc with B, sc2tog with D, sc in

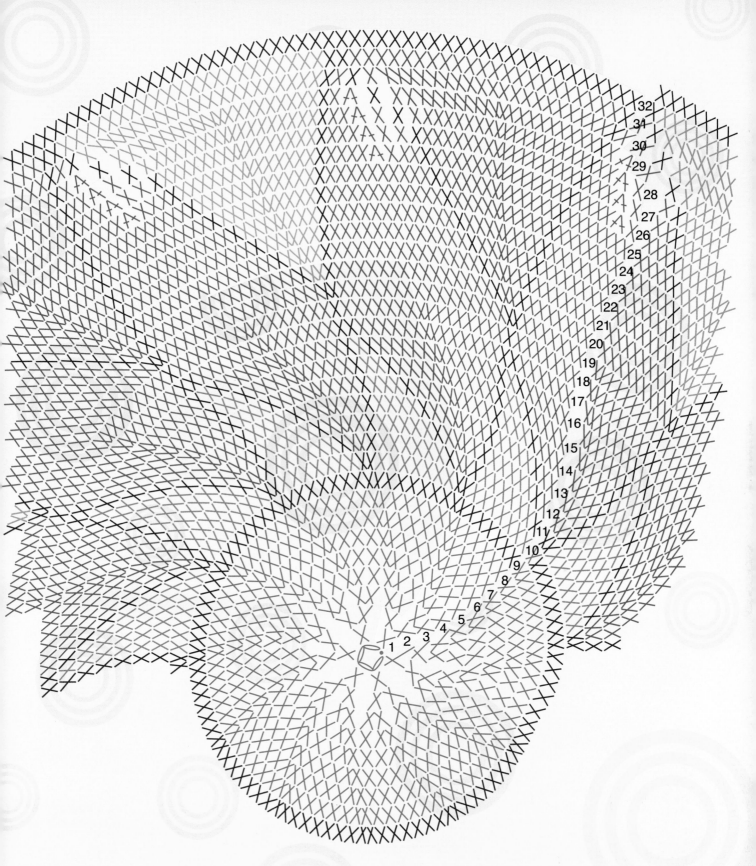

next sc with D, sc in next sc with B, sc in next 9 sc with F, 2 sc in next sc with F, sc in next 9 sc with F, sc in next sc with B; repeat from * 5 more times; sc in first sc with D.

Round 30 *Sc in next sc with D, sc in next sc with B, sc in next 21 sc with E, sc in next sc with B, sc in next sc with D, sc in next sc with B, sc in next 21 sc with F, sc in next sc with B; repeat from * 5 more times; sc in first sc with D.

Round 31 *Sc in next sc with B, sc in next 22 sc with E, sc in next 2 sc with B, sc in next 22 sc with F, sc in next sc with B; repeat from * 5 more times—288 sc.

Round 32 *With B throughout, sc in next 57 sc, cut one carried thread; repeat from * 4 more times; sc in next 3 sc; join with sl st in first sc. Fasten off, leaving a long end.

Finishing

Weave in ends. Block with a steam iron.

beaded Basket

Yarn
AUNT LYDIA'S *Fashion Crochet*
Thread, Size 3, 150yd/137m balls (cotton)
- 1 ball #0377 Tan (A)
- 1 ball #0226 Natural (B)
- 1 ball #0065 Warm Teal (C)

Crochet hook
Size 1 (2.75mm) steel crochet hook *or size to obtain gauge*

Notions
#8 seed beads by Fire Mountain Gems and Beads:
60g Transparent Root Beer, 118g Transparent Clear and 59g Opaque Turquoise
3 heavy beading needles
Stitch marker

Stitched in tapestry crochet, this lidded basket is loaded with beads and bursting with color. Give this new technique a try—you'll love the unique results.

Stitch Glossary
BBsc (back bead sc) Insert hook in specified st, slide a bead up next to hook, yo and draw up a lp, yo and draw through both lps on hook. Bead will lie at back of st.

Finished Measurements
Basket with lid 5"/12.5cm diameter x 3½"/9cm high.
Basket 4¼"/11cm diameter x 3"/7.5cm high.
Lid 5"/12.5cm diameter x 1¼"/3.18cm high.

Gauge
Rounds 1–5 = 1½"/4cm diameter
Remember to check gauge for best results!

How to Make a Gauge Swatch
With A, ch 4; join with sl st in first ch to form a ring.
Round 1 Work 6 sc in ring while carrying tail—6 sc.
Round 2 While carrying B, 2 sc in each st around—12 sc.
Round 3 Repeat Round 2—24 sc.
Round 4 *Sc in next st, 2 sc in next st; repeat from * 11 more times—36 sc.
Round 5 Sc in each st around. Swatch should measure approx 1½"/4cm diameter. Adjust hook size if necessary to obtain correct gauge.

Notes
1 This project is worked as a spiral. To keep track of where each round ends, place stitch marker in top of last st of round. Remove stitch marker from last st and place it in new last st at end of each round.

2 To carry nonworking thread, lay it over top two lps of sts on previous round and crochet as usual, placing carried thread inside st being worked. Hold carried thread in place with thumb.

3 To change colors, work st until 2 lps rem on hook, drop working thread, yo with carried thread and draw through both lps on hook.

4 Tapestry crochet sts are worked by carrying nonworking thread over top two lps of sts in round below while working sts over carried thread, changing colors as necessary.

Basket
With beading needle, string 702 Transparent Root Beer beads onto A, 1,152 Clear beads onto B, and 576 Turquoise beads onto C. Push beads down on thread, leaving 1yd/91cm long piece without beads near hook.
With A, ch 4; join with sl st in first ch to form a ring.
Round 1 Work 6 BBsc in ring while carrying tail—6 BBsc. Cut tail of A close to work and start to carry B.
Note On rounds 2–11, tapestry crochet with A while carrying B inside sts being worked.
Round 2 Work 2 BBsc in each st around—12 BBsc.
Round 3 Repeat Round 2—24 BBsc.
Round 4 *BBsc in next st, 2 BBsc in next st; repeat from * 11 more times—36 BBsc.
Round 5 BBsc in each st around.
Round 6 *BBsc in next 2 sts, 2 BBsc in next st; repeat from * 11 more times—48 BBsc.
Round 7 *BBsc in next 3 sts, 2 BBsc in next st; repeat from * 11 more times—60 BBsc.
Round 8 *BBsc in next 4 sts, 2 BBsc in next st; repeat from * 11 more times—72 BBsc.
Round 9 *BBsc in next 5 sts, 2 BBsc in next st; repeat from * 11 more times—84 BBsc.
Round 10 BBsc in each st around.
Round 11 *BBsc in next 6 sts, 2 BBsc in next st; repeat from * 11 more times—96 BBsc.
Note Refer to Chart 1. Rounds 12–35 correspond to the motif on the side of the basket (read from right to left and bottom to top). Continue to work in tapestry crochet, changing colors as necessary and carrying nonworking thread on top of sts in round below.
Round 12 *1 BBsc with B, 3 BBsc with A; repeat from * 23 more times.
Round 13 *2 BBsc with B, 2 BBsc with A; repeat from * 23 more times.
Round 14 *3 BBsc with B, 1 BBsc with A; repeat from * 23

more times.

Round 15 While carrying A, BBsc with B in each st around.

Round 16 Repeat Round 15. At end of round, cut A close to work and start carrying C.

Round 17 While carrying C, BBsc with B in each st around.

Round 18 *1 BBsc with C, 3 BBsc with B; repeat from * 23 more times.

Round 19 *2 BBsc with C, 2 BBsc with B; repeat from * 23 more times.

Round 20 *3 BBsc with C, 1 BBsc with B; repeat from * 23 more times.

Rounds 21–23 While carrying B, BBsc with C in each st around.

Round 24 *1 BBsc with B, 3 BBsc with C; repeat from * 23 more times.

Round 25 *2 BBsc with B, 2 BBsc with C; repeat from * 23 more times.

Round 26 *3 BBsc with B, 1 BBsc with C; repeat from * 23 more times.

Round 27 While carrying C, BBsc with B in each st around.

Round 28 Repeat Round 27. String 432 Transparent Root Beer beads onto A.

Cut C close to work and start carrying A.

Round 29 While carrying A, BBsc with B in each st around.

Round 30 *1 BBsc with A, 3 BBsc with B; repeat from * 23 more times.

Round 31 *2 BBsc with A, 2 BBsc with B; repeat from * 23 more times.

Round 32 *3 BBsc with A, 1 BBsc with B; repeat from * 23 more times.

Rounds 33–35 While carrying B, BBsc with A in each st around.

Round 36 With A and B held tog, sc in each st around. Fasten off.

Lid

With beading needle, string 1,098 Transparent Clear beads onto B and 540 Turquoise beads onto C. Push beads down on thread, leaving 1yd/91.5cm long piece without beads near hook.

With B, ch 4; join with sl st in first ch to form a ring.

Round 1 Work 6 BBsc in ring while carrying tail—6 BBsc. Cut tail of B close to work and start to carry C.

Note On Rounds 2–12, tapestry crochet with B while carrying C under sts being worked.

Rounds 2–11 With B, work same as rounds 2–11 on basket.

Round 12 *BBsc in next 7 sts, 2 BBsc in next st; repeat from * 11 more times—108 BBsc.

Refer to Chart 2. Rounds 13–21 correspond to the motif on the side of the lid (read from right to left and bottom to top). Continue to work in tapestry crochet, changing colors as necessary and carrying nonworking thread on top of sts in round below.

Round 13 *1 BBsc with C, 8 BBsc with B; repeat from * around 11 more times.

Round 14 *2 BBsc with C, 7 BBsc with B; repeat from * around 11 more times.

Round 15 *3 BBsc with C, 6 BBsc with B; repeat from * around 11 more times.

Round 16 *4 BBsc with C, 5 BBsc with B; repeat from * around 11 more times.

Round 17 *5 BBsc with C, 4 BBsc with B; repeat from * around 11 more times.

Round 18 *6 BBsc with C, 3 BBsc with B; repeat from * around 11 more times.

Round 19 *7 BBsc with C, 2 BBsc with B; repeat from * around 11 more times.

Round 20 *8 BBsc with C, 1 BBsc with B; repeat from * around 11 more times.

Round 21 While carrying B, BBsc with C in each st around.

Round 22 With B and C held tog, sc in each st around. Fasten off.

Finishing

Weave in all ends. Turn work bead side out.

Blocking

Cover each piece with a towel and carefully block with a steam iron. Be careful not to use too much heat, which might break the beads.

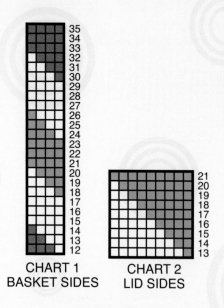

CHART 1
BASKET SIDES

CHART 2
LID SIDES

CHART KEY

■ = BBsc in Tan (A)
□ = BBsc in Natural (B)
▨ = BBsc in Warm Teal (C)

sweet Sachets

Yarn
AUNT LYDIA'S *Fashion Crochet Thread*, Size 3, 150yd/137m balls (cotton)
• 1 ball # 226 Natural

Crochet hook
Size B/1 (2.25mm) crochet hook *or size to obtain gauge*

Notions
Fabric of choice, 9"/23cm x 5"/12.5cm piece
Lavender or potpourri to fill sachet, or fiberfill
Sewing needle
Sewing thread to match fabric
Stitch marker or safety pin
Straight pins
Sewing machine (optional)
Yarn needle

Jack Deutsch

These petite sachets are perfect for filet first–timers—practice your skills and finish a pretty project in no time.

Stitch Glossary
open mesh Ch 2, sk next 2 sts, dc in next dc.
beg open mesh Ch 5, sk next 2 sts, dc in next dc.
block (over open mesh) Work 2 dc in next ch–2 sp, dc in next dc.
block (over block) Dc in next 3 dc.
picot Ch 2, sl st in 2nd ch from hook.

Finished Measurements
4¼"/11cm square plus border.

Gauge
Square = 4¼"/11cm
Gauge is not essential for this project!

Sachet
Square (make 2)
Ch 38.
Note Odd numbered rows on chart are worked from right to left. Even numbered rows on chart are worked from left to right.
Row 1 (RS) Dc in 8th ch from hook; *ch 2, sk next 2 chs, dc in next ch; repeat from * across—11 open mesh. Turn.
Rows 2–14 Beg with Row 2 of chart, work beg open mesh, open mesh and blocks as per chart. Work beg open mesh for first blank square on each row. Turn at end of each row. Fasten off after last row on first square only. Do not fasten off second square.

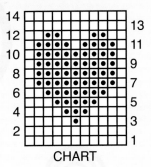

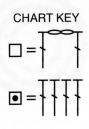

CHART KEY

CHART

Blocking
Remove lp from hook on second square and place a stitch marker or safety pin in lp to keep from unraveling. Pin and block each square to 4¼"/11cm square. Allow to dry.

Lining
Fold fabric in half with right sides tog into 5"/12.5cm x 4½"/11.5cm square. Pin raw edges tog. With sewing needle (or sewing machine) and matching thread, sew seam with ½"/1.25cm seam allowance along 2 unfolded edges. Turn fabric right side out. Stuff lightly with fiberfill. Turn raw edges under ½"/1.25cm to inside and pin tog. Sew opening closed.

Joining
Place squares with wrong sides tog, aligning edges and hearts. Insert hook in removed lp from second square, ch

graphic lace Curtain

Yarn
AUNT LYDIA'S *Fashion Crochet*
Thread, Size 3, each ball approx
150yd/137m (cotton)
• 6 balls #226 Natural

Crochet hook
Size D/3 (3.25mm) crochet hook *or size to obtain gauge*

Notions
Stitch marker
Yarn needle

This fresh take on an old–world favorite brings sophisti-cated charm to any window. Easy repeats and minimal shaping make it a perfect project for crochet newbies.

Finished Measurements
Approx 36"/91.5cm wide x 24"/61cm high.

Stitch Glossary
open block Ch 1, skip next ch–1 space or dc, dc in next dc.
closed block Dc in next ch–1 space or dc, dc in next dc.
dc2tog (double crochet 2 sts together) [Yarn over, insert hook in next st, yarn over and draw up a loop, yarn over and draw through 2 loops on hook] twice, yarn over and draw through all 3 loops on hook.

Gauge
21 sts and 9 rows = 4"/10cm over filet pattern using size D/3 (3.25mm) crochet hook.
Remember to check gauge for best results!

How To Make A Gauge Swatch
Ch 23.
Row 1 Dc in 4th ch from hook (beg ch counts as first dc) and in each remaining ch across—21 dc (10 closed blocks).
Row 2 Ch 3 (counts as first dc), turn, dc in each st across.
Row 3 Ch 3, turn, dc in next 4 sts (2 closed blocks made), [ch 1, sk next st, dc in next st (open block made)] 6 times, dc in next 4 sts—6 open blocks and 2 closed blocks on each end.
Rows 4–8 Ch 3, turn, dc in next 4 sts, [ch 1, sk next ch–1 space, dc in next dc] 6 times, dc in next 4 sts.
Row 9 Ch 3, turn, dc in each ch–1 space and dc across. Resulting gauge swatch should measure approx 4" x 4"/10cm x 10cm. Adjust hook size if necessary to obtain correct gauge.

Special Technique
Working Filet Chart
1 Read right–side rows from right to left, read wrong–side rows from left to right.
2 Work an open block when an empty square is encoun-

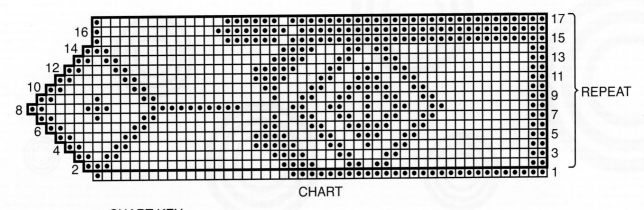

CHART

CHART KEY
☐ = closed block: dc in next ch-1 space or dc, dc in next dc
▣ = open block: ch 1, skip next ch-1 space or dc, dc in next dc

tered, and a closed block when a filled square is encountered.

3 To increase one block at the end of a row, work 2 additional double crochet stitches in the last stitch. To increase one block at the beg of a row, work 2 additional double crochet stitches in the first stitch.

4 To decrease one block at the end of a row, work to last 3 stitches then work a dc2tog inserting the hook into the next and last stitches (sk center stitch). To decrease one block at the beg of a row, ch 3 and turn as usual, sk next stitch and continue in pattern, do not work in the top of the turning ch at the end of the next row.

Curtain

Ch 109.

Foundation Row 1 Dc in 4th ch from hook (beg ch counts as first dc) and in each remaining ch across—107 dc (53 closed blocks).

Foundation Row 2 Ch 3 (counts as first dc here and throughout), turn, dc in each st across. Place a marker on this side to indicate wrong side of curtain.

Work Chart

Chart Row 1 (RS) Ch 3, turn, dc in next 66 sts, [ch 1, sk next st, dc in next st (open block made)] 20 times, 2 dc in same (last) st (one block increase made)—54 blocks.
Work Rows 2–17 of chart four times, then repeat Rows 2–14 of chart.
Next Row (RS) Repeat Chart Row 1.
Last 2 Rows Ch 3, turn, dc in each dc and ch–1 space across.
Fasten off.

Finishing

Border

With right side facing, join thread in upper corner, to work along top of curtain.
Round 1 Ch 4 (counts as dc, ch 1), [dc in corner, ch 1] 3 times; working in ends of rows across top of curtain, *dc in end of next row, ch 1; repeat from * across to next corner; [dc in corner, ch 1] 4 times; pivot to work along side of curtain, **sk next st, dc in next st, ch 1; repeat from ** to next corner; [dc in corner, ch 1] 4 times; pivot to work in ends of rows along lower edge of curtain, *dc in end of next row, ch 1; repeat from * across to next corner; [dc in corner, ch 1] 4 times; pivot to work along side of curtain, ***sk next st, dc in next st, ch 1; repeat from *** to end; join with sl st in 3rd ch of beg ch. Fasten off.

Top Edging

With right side facing, join thread in upper corner ch–1 space, to work along top of curtain.
Row 1 Ch 3 (counts as dc), sk same ch–1 space as join, 2 dc in each ch–1 space across to last ch–1 space, dc in last ch–1 space. Fasten off.
Weave in all ends.

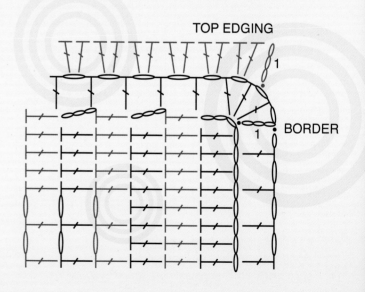

TOP EDGING

BORDER

Yarn

AUNT LYDIA'S *Classic Crochet
Thread*, Size 10, each ball approx
350yd/320m (cotton)
• 1 ball #001 White
• 1 ball #493 French Rose
• 1 ball #494 Victory Red
Note 1 ball will make several hearts.

Crochet hook

Size 6 (1.8mm) steel crochet hook *or size
to obtain gauge*

Notions

Yarn needle
Spray starch

Spread a little love to your special someone by embellishing a gift with this crocheted classic.

Stitch Glossary

Beg cl (beg cluster) Ch 3, [yo, insert hook in indicated space and draw up a lp, yo and draw through 2 lps on hook] twice, yo and draw through all 3 lps on hook.

Finished Measurements

Approx 4½"/11.5cm wide x 5"/12.5cm high.

Gauge

First 2 rounds of motif = 2"/5cm in diameter using Size 6 (1.8mm) steel crochet hook.
Gauge is not essential for this project!

Heart

Ch 4; join with sl st in first ch to form a ring.
Round 1 (flower round) Ch 3, [yo, insert hook in ring and draw up a lp, yo and draw through 2 lps on hook] twice, yo and draw through all 3 lps on hook (Beg cl made—counts as 1 cluster), ch 5, [(yo, insert hook in ring and draw up a lp, yo and draw through 2 lps on hook) 3 times, yo and draw through all 4 lps on hook (cluster made), ch 5] 5 times; join with sl st in top of Beg cl—6 clusters.
Round 2 Sl st into first ch–5 sp, ch 3 (counts as dc), 6 dc in same sp; ch 1, [7 dc in next ch–5 sp, ch 1] 5 times; join with sl st in top of beg ch–3—42 dc and 6 ch–1 sp.
Round 3 Ch 3, sk next dc, sc in next dc, [ch 3, sk next dc or ch–1 sp, sc in next dc] around to last ch–1 sp, sk last ch–1 sp; join with sl st in st at base of beg ch–3—23 ch–3 sp.
Round 4 (form heart) Ch 3, dc in next ch–sp, ch 3, tr in next ch–sp, ch 3, [dtr, ch 3, dtr] in next ch–sp, ch 3, [tr, ch 3, dc] in next ch–sp; ch 3, dc in next ch–sp, ch 3, [hdc in

next ch–sp, ch 2] 6 times; [dc, ch 3, dc] in next ch–sp (bottom point made); [ch 2, hdc in next ch–sp] 6 times; ch 3, dc in next ch–sp, ch 3; [dc, ch 3, tr] in next ch–sp, ch 3, [dtr, ch 3, dtr] in next ch–sp, ch 3, tr in next ch–sp, ch 3, dc in next ch–sp, ch 3; join with sl st in st at base of beg ch–3—29 ch–sp.

Round 5 Sl st into first ch–sp, [ch 3, sc in next ch–sp] 3 times, ch 4 (upper edge of heart), sc in next ch–sp, [ch 3, sc in next ch–sp] 4 times, [ch 2, sc in next ch–sp] 5 times,

ch 2, [sc, ch 3, sc] in bottom point, ch 2; [sc in next ch–sp, ch 2] 5 times, [sc in next ch–sp, ch 3] 4 times, sc in next ch–sp, ch 4 (upper edge of heart), [sc in next ch–sp, ch 3] 3 times, sk last ch–3 sp; join with sl st in beg sl st.

Round 6 (see diagram) [Sl st, Beg cl] in each ch–sp to first upper edge ch–4 sp, [sl st, Beg cl] twice in next ch–4 sp, [sl st, Beg cl] in each ch–sp to next upper edge ch–4 sp, [sl st, Beg cl] twice in next ch–4 sp, [sl st, Beg cl] in each ch–sp to end; join with sl st in beg sl st—31 Beg cl.

Fasten off.

Finishing

Weave in all ends. Lightly coat heart with spray starch and press.

lovely Dishcloths

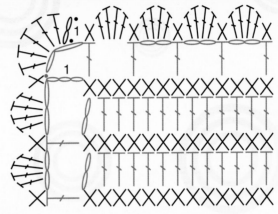

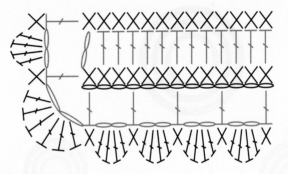

Yarn
AUNT LYDIA'S *Fashion Crochet*
Thread, Size 3, each ball approx 150yd/137m
(cotton)
• 1 ball #006 Scarlet (A)
• 1 ball #775 Warm Rose (B)

Crochet Hook
Size E/4 (3.5mm) crochet hook *or size to obtain gauge*

Notions
Yarn needle

Wrap these sweet cloths with some pretty soaps for a heartfelt gift any time of the year.

Finished Measurements
Approx 9"/23cm square.

Gauge
25 sts and 18 rows = 4"/10cm over pattern as established using size E/4 (3.5mm) crochet hook.
Gauge is not essential for this project!

How To Make A Gauge Swatch
With A or B, ch 26.
Row 1 Sc in 2nd ch from hook and in each ch across—25 sc.
Row 2 Ch 2 (does not count as a st), turn, dc in each sc across.
Row 3 Ch 1, turn, sc in each dc across.
Repeat Rows 2 and 3 fourteen more times, then repeat Row 2. Resulting gauge swatch should measure approx 4 x 4"/10 x 10cm. Adjust hook size if necessary to obtain correct gauge.

Notes
1 To change color, work last stitch of old color until there are 2 loops remaining on hook. Yarn over with new color and draw through loops on hook to complete stitch.

2 When changing color, drop old color and pick up new color; do not carry colors across back of work.

3 Refer to chart for clarification when working color change pattern.

Dishcloth 1
With A, ch 48.
Row 1 Sc in 2nd ch from hook and in each ch across—47 sc.
Row 2 Ch 2 (does not count as a stitch), turn, dc in each sc across.
Row 3 Ch 1, turn, sc in each dc across.
Rows 4–6 Repeat Rows 2 and 3 once, then repeat Row 2 once more.
Row 7 Ch 1, turn, sc in first 23 dc; change to B, sc in next dc; change to A, sc in last 23 dc.
Row 8 Ch 2, turn, dc in first 22 sc; change to B, dc in next 3 sc; change to A, dc in last 22 sc.
Row 9 Ch 1, turn, sc in first 21 dc; change to B, sc in next 5 dc; change to A, sc in last 21 dc.
Row 10 Ch 2, dc in first 20 sc; change to B, dc in next 7 sc; change to A, dc in last 20 sc.
Row 11 Ch 1, turn, sc in first 19 dc; change to B, dc in next 9 dc; change to A, sc in last 19 dc.
Row 12 Ch 2, turn, dc in first 18 sc; change to B, dc in next 11 sc; change to A, dc in last 18 sc.
Row 13 Ch 1, turn, sc in first 17 dc; change to B, dc in next

13 dc; change to A, sc in last 17 dc.

Row 14 Ch 2, turn, dc in first 16 sc; change to B, dc in next 15 sc; change to A, dc in last 16 sc.

Row 15 Ch 1, turn, sc in first 15 dc; change to B, dc in next 17 dc; change to A, sc in last 15 dc.

Row 16 Ch 2, turn, dc in first 14 sc; change to B, dc in next 19 sc; change to A, dc in last 14 sc.

Row 17 Ch 1, turn, sc in first 13 dc; change to B, dc in next 21 dc; change to A, sc in last 13 dc.

Row 18 Ch 2, turn, dc in first 12 sc; change to B, dc in next 23 sc; change to A, dc in last 12 sc.

Row 19 Ch 1, turn, sc in first 11 dc; change to B, dc in next 25 dc; change to A, sc in last 11 dc.

Row 20 Ch 2, turn, dc in first 11 sc; change to B, dc in next 25 sc; change to A, dc in last 11 sc.

Rows 21–23 Repeat Rows 19 and 20 once, then repeat Row 19 once more.

Row 24 Ch 2, turn, dc in first 12 sc; change to B, dc in next 11 sc; change to A, dc in next sc; change to B, dc in next

11 sc; change to A, dc in last 12 sc.

Row 25 Ch 1, turn, sc in first 13 dc; change to B, sc in next 9 dc; change to A, sc in next 3 dc; change to B, sc in next 9 dc; change to A, sc in last 13 dc.

Row 26 Ch 2, turn, dc in first 14 sc; change to B, dc in next 7 sc; change to A, dc in next 5 sc; change to B, dc in next 7 sc; change to A, dc in last 14 sc.

Row 27 Ch 1, turn, sc in first 15 dc; change to B, sc in next 5 dc; change to A, sc in next 7 dc; change to B, sc in next 5 dc; change to A, sc in last 15 dc.

Row 28 With A, ch 2, turn, dc in each sc across.

Row 29 With A, ch 1, turn, sc in each dc across.

Rows 30–33 Repeat Rows 28 and 29 twice.

Fasten off B. Do not fasten off A.

Border

Round 1 Pivot work to work in ends of rows along side, with A, ch 5 (counts as dc and ch 2), [sk next dc row, dc in next sc row, ch 2] across to next corner; [dc, ch 2, dc] in corner; pivot work to work in free loops along opposite side of foundation ch, ch 2, [sk 2 ch, dc in next ch, ch 2] across to next corner; [dc, ch 2, dc] in corner; pivot work to work in ends of rows along side, ch 2, [sk next dc row, dc in next sc row, ch 2] across to next corner; [dc, ch 2, dc] in corner; pivot work to work in sc of last row, ch 2, [sk 2 sc, dc in next sc, ch 2] across to last corner; [dc, ch 2] in same sp as beg ch–5; join with sl st in 3rd ch of beg ch–5.

Fasten off A.

Ruffle edging

Join B with sl st in any corner ch–2 sp.

Round 1 Ch 3, 5 dc in same ch–2 sp, sc in next dc, *[4 dc in next ch–2 sp, sc in next dc] across to corner ch–2 sp, 6 dc in corner ch–2 sp, sc in next dc; repeat from * around; join with sl st in top of beg ch.

Fasten off.

Finishing

Weave in all ends.

Dishcloth 2

Work same as Dishcloth 1, reversing A and B throughout.

CHART

CHART KEY
☐ = Warm Rose (B)
■ = Scarlet (A)
Odd-numbered rows in sc
Even-numbered rows in dc

Yarn

AUNT LYDIA'S *Cable Crochet Thread,*
Size 3, 3oz/87g balls, each approx
200yd/183m balls (cotton)
• 1 ball #0226 Natural)

Crochet Hook

Size F/5 (3.75mm) crochet hook *or any size to
obtain correct gauge*

Notions

Yarn needle
Fabric stiffener (or 2 cups sugar, 1 cup water,
tongs and 2–qt saucepan)
Large mixing bowl, approx 10"/25cm diameter
Plastic wrap
Craft paper or newspaper

Rose Callahan

A guaranteed conversation–starter, this chunky starched bowl makes a stunning display piece. Craft one for yourself, or gift it to someone special.

Finished Measurments

Stiffened bowl is approximately 10"/25cm diameter x 4"/10cm high.

Gauge

Rounds 1 and 2 = 2½"/6.5cm diameter
Remember to check gauge for best results!

Bowl

Ch 7; join with sl st to form a ring.

Round 1 Ch 5 (counts as first dc and ch–2 sp), [dc in ring, ch 2] 7 times; join with sl st in 3rd ch of beg ch–5—8 dc and 8 ch–2 sps.

Round 2 Sl st in next dc, ch 3 (counts as first dc), 4 dc in next ch–2 sp; *dc in next dc, 4 dc in next ch–2 sp; repeat from * around; join with sl st in 3rd ch of beg ch–3—40 dc.

Round 3 Ch 3 (counts as first dc), sc in next 2 dc, dc in next dc, ch 5, sk next dc; *dc in next dc, sc in next 2 dc, dc in next dc, ch 5, sk next dc; repeat from * around; join—16 dc, 16 sc and 8 ch–5 sps.

Round 4 *Ch 5, sk next 2 sc, sl st in next dc, (sc, 5 dc, sc) in next ch–5 sp (petal made)**; sl st in next dc; repeat from * around, ending final repeat at **; join with sl st in joining sl st on round 3—8 petals and 8 ch–5 sps.

Round 5 Sl st in next 3 chs, ch 9 (counts as first dc and ch–6 sp), sc in 3rd dc of next petal; * ch 6, dc in 3rd ch of next ch–5 sp, ch 6, sc in 3rd dc of next petal; repeat from * around; ch 6; join with sl st in 3rd ch of beg ch–9—8 dc, 8 sc and 16 ch–6 sps.

Round 6 Sl st in next 3 chs, ch 1, sc in same ch–sp; * ch 10, sc in next ch–6 sp; repeat from * around; ch 10; join with sl st in first sc—16 sc and 16 ch–10 sps.

Round 7 Ch 1; * (sc, 3 dc, ch 1, 3 dc, sc) in next ch–10 sp (petal made); repeat from * around; join—16 petals.

Round 8 Ch 8 (counts as first tr and ch–4 sp), sk next 3 sts, sc in next ch–1 sp; * ch 4, sk next 4 sts, tr in sp between 2 petals, ch 4, sk next 4 sts, sc in next ch–1 sp; repeat from * around; ch 4; join with sl st in 4th ch of beg ch–8—16 tr, 16 sc and 32 ch–4 sps.

Round 9 Sl st in next ch–4 sp, ch 3 (counts as first dc); 3 dc in same ch–4 sp; * 4 dc in next ch–4 sp; repeat from * around; join with sl st in 3rd ch of beg ch–3—128 dc.

Round 10 Ch 4 (counts as first dc and ch–1 sp), sk next dc; * dc in next dc, ch 1, sk next dc; repeat from * around; join with sl st in 3rd ch of beg ch–4—64 dc and 64 ch–1 sps.

Round 11 Ch 1, sc in same ch as joining, sc in next ch, sc in next dc, sc in next ch; * ch 6, sk next dc and next ch **; [sc in next dc, sc in next ch] 3 times; repeat from * around, ending final repeat at **; sc in next dc, sc in next ch; join with sl st in first sc—96 sc and 16 ch–6 sps.

Round 12 Sl st in next 2 sc; * ch 1, [dc, ch 1] 5 times in next ch–6 sp (petal made), sk next sc, sl st in next sc, ch 4**; sk next 2 sc, sl st in next sc; repeat from * around, ending final repeat at **; sk next 2 sl sts; join with sl st in next sl st—16 petals and 16 ch–4 sps. Fasten off.

Finishing

Weave in all ends.

Stiffening Bowl

To stiffen bowl, you may use a commercial fabric stiffener and follow the instructions on the label, or use the homemade sugar–and–water method below. To start, cover your work surface with plastic wrap or a garbage bag and several sheets of newspaper. Place large mixing bowl

upside–down on top of paper and cover bowl with plastic wrap to make clean–up easier. Experiment with placement of crocheted bowl on top of mixing bowl before you get started—a smaller/taller bowl will yield a bowl that ruffles at the top, a larger/wider bowl will yield a bowl that is flatter and shorter.

Homemade Stiffener

Combine 2 cups sugar and 1 cup water in sauce-pan. Heat on stove just until sugar is dissolved. Be careful as solution is very hot! Remove pan from heat and soak crocheted bowl in solution. Let cool slightly. With tongs, remove crocheted bowl from saucepan and drape over mixing bowl, shaping as desired. Once piece has sufficiently cooled, shape bowl further with fingers. Let dry for at least 3 days. When thread returns to normal color, bowl is stiff-ened and ready for use.

Yarn
AUNT LYDIA'S *Fashion Crochet Thread*, Size 5, each ball approx 0.9oz/26g 100yd/91m (cotton)
•6 balls #4105 Silver/Silver

Crochet Hooks
Size D/3 (3.25mm) crochet hook *or size to obtain gauge*

Additional
Polyester fiberfill
Yarn needle

Crocheted in metallic thread, this "silver" set makes a charmingly crafty addition to teatime playdates. Stitch it up quick for a sweet gift—and don't forget the cookies!

Stitch Glossary
Bsc (Back Post single crochet) Insert hook from back to front to back again around post of indicated stitch, yarn over and draw up a loop, yarn over and draw through both loops on hook.

sc2tog (single crochet 2 stitches together) [Insert hook in next st, yarn over and draw up a loop] twice, yarn over and draw through all 3 loops on hook.

Finished Measurements
Teapot Approx 5"/12.5cm diameter x 6"/15cm tall, excluding spout and handle .

Teacup Approx 2¾"/7cm diameter (at widest point) x 2¼"/5.5cm tall.

Saucer Approx 3"/7.5cm diameter.

Gauge
Rounds 1–8 = 4"/10cm diameter over sc, holding 2 strands of thread together throughout. *Remember to check gauge for best results!*

How To Make A Gauge Swatch
Holding 2 strands of thread together, work Rounds 1–8 of teapot.

Resulting gauge swatch should measure approx 4"/10cm diameter. Adjust hook size if necessary to obtain correct gauge.

Note
1 Two strands of thread are held together throughout.
2 Exact gauge is not critical. Work tightly to ensure that stuffing does not show through stitches.

Teapot
Holding 2 strands of thread together, ch 3; join with sl st in first ch to form a ring.

Round 1 (RS) Ch 1, work 8 sc in ring; join with sl st in first sc—8 sc.

Round 2 Ch 1, 2 sc in each sc around—16 sc.

Round 3 Ch 1, [sc in next sc, 2 sc in next sc] 8 times; join with sl st in first sc—24 sc.

Round 4 Ch 1, [sc in next 2 sc, 2 sc in next sc] 8 times; join with sl st in first sc—32 sc.

Round 5 Ch 1, [sc in next 3 sc, 2 sc in next sc] 8 times; join with sl st in first sc—40 sc.

Round 6 Ch 1, [sc in next 4 sc, 2 sc in next sc] 8 times; join with sl st in first sc—48 sc.

Round 7 Ch 1, [sc in next 5 sc, 2 sc in next sc] 8 times; join with sl st in first sc—56 sc.

Round 8 Ch 1, [sc in next 6 sc, 2 sc in next sc] 8 times; join with sl st in first sc—64 sc.

Round 9 Ch 1, [sc in next 7 sc, 2 sc in next sc] 8 times; join with sl st in first sc—72 sc.

Rounds 10 and 11 Ch 1, sc in each sc around; join with sl st in first sc.

Round 12 Sk joined st, sk next 2 sts, 5 dc in next st, sk next 2 sts, [sl st in next st, sk next 2 sts, 5 dc in next st, sk next 2 sts] 11 times; join with sl st in join of previous round—12 shells.

Round 13 Ch 3 (counts as first dc here and throughout), 2 dc in same st as join, [sk next 2 dc, sl st in next dc (center dc of 5–dc group), sk next 2 dc, 5 dc in next sl st] 11 times, sk next 2 dc, sl st in next dc, sk next 2 dc, 2 dc in same st as beg; join with sl st in top of beg ch.

Rounds 14–20 Repeat Rows 12 and 13 three times; then repeat Row 12 once more.

Rounds 21 and 22 Ch 1, sc in each st around; join with sl st in first sc—72 sc.

Round 23 Ch 1, [sc in next 7 sts, sc2tog] 8 times; join with sl st in first sc—64 sc.

Round 24 Ch 1, [sc in next 6 sts, sc2tog] 8 times; join with sl st in first sc—56 sc.

Round 25 Ch 1, [sc in next 5 sts, sc2tog] 8 times; join with sl st in first sc—48 sc.

Round 26 Ch 1, [sc in next 4 sts, sc2tog] 8 times; join with sl st in first sc—40 sc. Fasten off.

Spout
Holding 2 strands of thread together, ch 20; join with sl st in first ch to form a ring.

Rose Callahan

Round 1 (right side) Ch 1, sc in each ch around; join with sl st in first sc—20 sc.

Round 2 Ch 1, sc in next 9 sc, sc2tog, sc in last 9 sc; join with sl st in first sc—19 sc.

Rounds 3–8 Ch 1, sc in each sc to the sc2tog, sc2tog, sc in each sc to the end; join with sl st in first sc—13 sc. Fasten off.

Handle
Holding 2 strands of thread together, ch 21.

Row 1 Sc in 2nd ch from hook and in each remaining ch across—20 sc. Rows 2–7 Ch 1, turn, sc in each sc across.
Fasten off.

Lid
Holding 2 strands of thread together, ch 3; join with sl st in first ch to form a ring.

Round 1 (right side) Ch 2, work 10 hdc in the ring; join with sl st in top of beg ch—10 hdc.

Round 2 Ch 2, 2 hdc in each hdc around; join with sl st in top of beg ch—20 hdc.

Round 3 Ch 2, [hdc in next hdc, 2 hdc in next hdc] 10 times; join with sl st in top of beg ch—30 hdc.

Round 4 Ch 2, [hdc in next 2 hdc, 2 hdc in next hdc] 10 times; join with sl st in top of beg ch—40 hdc. Fasten off.

Knob

Holding 2 strands of thread together, ch 3; join with sl st in first ch to form a ring.

Round 1 (RS) Work 8 sc in ring; do not join, work in a continuous spiral.

Round 2 2 sc in each sc around—16 sc.

Round 3 Sc in each sc around.

Round 4 (Sc2tog) 8 times; sl st in next st. Fasten off, leaving a long tail.

Teacup (make 2)

Base (make 4—2 for each cup)

Holding 2 strands of thread together, ch 3; join with sl st in first ch to form a ring.

Round 1 (RS) Ch 2, work 13 hdc in ring; join with sl st in top of beg ch.

Round 2 Ch 2, [2 hdc in next hdc, hdc in next hdc] 6 times, 2 hdc in last hdc; join with sl st in top of beg ch—20 hdc.

Round 3 Ch 1, [2 sc in next hdc, sc in next hdc] around; join with sl st in first sc—30 sc. Fasten off.

Cup

Holding 2 strands of thread together, ch 3; join with sl st in first ch to form a ring.

Round 1 (inside of cup) Ch 1, work 7 sc in ring; join with sl st in first sc.

Round 2 Ch 1, 2 sc in each sc around; join with sl st in first sc—14 sc.

Round 3 Ch 2, [sc in next sc, 2 sc in next sc] 7 times; join with sl st in first sc—21 sc. Fasten off.
Flip piece over.

Round 4 From outside of cup, holding 2 strands of thread together, draw up a loop of thread in any sc of Round 3, ch 1, BPsc around each sc around; join with sl st in first sc.

Round 5 Ch 1, [sc in next 2 sc, 2 sc in next sc] 7 times; join with sl st in first sc—28 sc.

Round 6 Ch 1, sc in each sc around; join with sl st in first sc.

Round 7 Ch 1, [sc in next 3 sc, 2 sc in next sc] 7 times; join with sl st in first sc—35 sc.

Round 8 Ch 1, [sc in next 4 sc, 2 sc in next sc] 7 times; join with sl st in first sc—42 sc.

Rounds 9–12 Ch 1, sc in each sc around; join with sl st in first sc.

Round 13 Ch 1, [sc in next 6 sc, 2 sc in next sc] 6 times—48 sc.

Round 14 Ch 1, sc in each st around; join with sl st in first sc.

Round 15 Ch 1, [sc in next 7 sc, 2 sc in next sc] 6 times—54 sc.

Round 16 Ch 1, sc in each st around; join with sl st in first sc.

Round 17 Sl st in each sc around. Fasten off.

Handle

Holding 2 strands of thread together, ch 17.

Row 1 Sc in 2nd ch from hook and in each remaining ch across—16 sc.

Rows 2 and 3 Ch 1, turn, sc in each sc across.
Fasten off.

Saucer (make 2)

Holding 2 strands of thread together, ch 3; join with sl st in first ch to form a ring.

Rounds 1–4 Work Rounds 1–4 of teapot lid.

Round 5 Ch 2, [hdc in next 3 hdc, 2 hdc in next hdc]; join with sl st in top of beg ch—50 hdc.
Fasten off.

Finishing

Assemble Teapot

Stuff knob with fiberfill. Weave the tail through the sts of the last round and pull tight. Thread tail onto yarn needle and sew knob to center of lid. Sew long edges of handle together and stuff tube with fiberfill. Sew one end of handle, over seam, to top round of shell section. Gently bend handle and sew other end to second round of shell section. Sew larger end of spout to opposite side of teapot, near top of shell section. Stuff pot with fiberfill and sew lid over opening at top.

Assemble Teacups

Sew long edges of handle together. Gently bend handle and sew ends, approx 1"/2.5cm apart, over side seam. Holding wrong sides together, sew edges of two bases together. Sew bottom of teacup to the base. Weave in all ends.

Tip

A sugar bowl would sweeten up this set. Simply make another teacup with two handles (sew one on each side), and stitch up another saucer with an extra round even in hdc. Sew a knob to the saucer to make a "lid", stuff the bowl and sew lid on top.

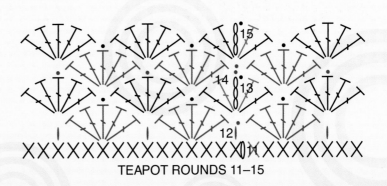

TEAPOT ROUNDS 11–15

coaster Comeback

This coaster is the center of an intricate and beautiful doily we found in our pattern archives. When we saw the heart motif, we knew it'd be a charming coaster—just right for last-minute Valentine's Day gifts. Sweet!

Stitch Glossary

dc2tog (dc 2 stitches together) [Yarn over, insert hook in next dc, yarn over and draw up a loop, yarn over and draw through 2 loops on hook] twice, yarn over and draw through all 3 loops on hook.

dc3tog (dc 3 stitches together) [Yarn over, insert hook in next dc, yarn over and draw up a loop, yarn over and draw through 2 loops on hook] 3 times, yarn over and draw through all 4 loops on hook.

Finished Meaurements

Approx 3½"/9cm diameter.

Note

One ball of thread makes approx 25–30 coasters.

Gauge

doily = 3½"/9cm diameter
Remember to check gauge for best results!

Doily

Ch 4; join with sl st to form a ring.
Round 1 (RS) Ch 5 (counts as dc and ch–2 sp), [dc in ring, ch 2] 5 times; join with sl st in 3rd ch of beg ch–5—6 dc and 6 ch–2 sps.
Round 2 Ch 3 (counts as dc now and throughout), 2 dc in same ch as joining, [ch 3, sk next ch–2 sp, 3 dc in next dc] 5 times; ch 3, sk next ch–2 sp; join with sl st in 3rd ch of beg ch–3—18 dc and 6 ch–3 sps.
Round 3 Ch 3, dc in same ch as joining, dc in next dc, 2 dc in next dc, [ch 3, sk next ch–3 sp, 2 dc in next dc, dc in next dc, 2 dc in next dc] 5 times; ch 3, sk next ch–3 sp; join—30 dc and 6 ch–3 sps.

Yarn

AUNT LYDIA'S *Classic Crochet Thread*, size 10, each ball approx 400yd/366m for white or 350yd/320m for colors (cotton) 1 ball each (or color of choice):
• #1 White
• #226 Natural
• #475 Dusty Rose
• #494 Victory Red
• #492 Burgundy

Crochet Hooks

Size 6/1.80mm steel crochet hook *or size to obtain gauge*

Additional

Yarn needles

Round 4 Ch 3, dc in same ch as joining, dc in next 3 dc, 2 dc in next dc, [ch 3, sk next ch–3 sp, 2 dc in next dc, dc in next 3 dc, 2 dc in next dc] 5 times; ch 3, sk next ch–3 sp; join—42 dc and 6 ch–3 sps.
Round 5 Ch 2, dc2tog, ch 3, sl st in next dc, ch 3, dc3tog, [ch 3, sl st in next ch–3 sp, ch 3, dc3tog, ch 3, sl st in next dc, ch 3, dc3tog] 5 times; ch 3, sl st in next ch–3 sp; ch 1, join with hdc in top of dc2tog (counts as ch–3 sp)—12 dc and 24 ch–3 sps.
Round 6 Ch 1, sc around post of hdc, ch 3; *sc in next ch–3 sp, ch 3; repeat from * around; join with sl st in first sc—24 ch–3 sps. Fasten off.

Finishing

Weave in ends.

Tip

All sorts of delightful decorations could be made using this pattern! Attach a mini doily to a card, put one in a square frame or stitch a few to a pillowcase.

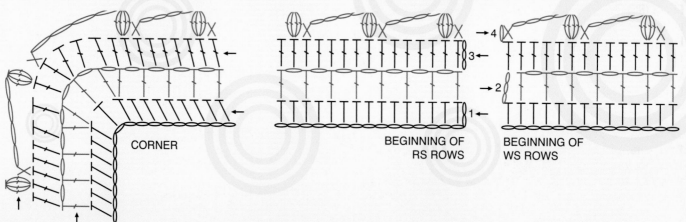

CORNER

BEGINNING OF
RS ROWS

BEGINNING OF
WS ROWS

4

3

2

1

dinner party Napkins

Set an elegant table with these stunning napkins. A set of them makes an heirloom–worthy wedding or housewarming gift.

Stitch Glossary
CL (cluster stitch) [Yarn over, insert hook into st and draw up a loop. Yarn over and draw through 2 loops on hook] 4 times, yarn over and draw through all 5 loops on hook.

Gauge
25 sts to 4"/10cm over dc using size 2 (2.25mm) steel crochet hook.
Lace trim measures approximately 1"/2.5cm wide using size 2 (2.25mm) steel crochet hook.
Remember to check gauge for best results!

How To Make A Gauge Swatch
Ch 28.
Row 1 (RS) Dc in 4th ch from hook and in each ch across—25 sts. Ch 3, turn.
Row 2 Dc in each st across. Ch 3, turn. Repeat row 2 four times more. Fasten off. Swatch should measure 4"/10cm wide. If necessary, adjust hook size to obtain correct gauge.

Lace Trim
With MC, ch 530.
Row 1 (RS) Working through back loops only, hdc in 3rd ch from hook and in each ch across—528 sts. Turn.
Row 2 Ch 4, skip first st, [dc in next st, ch 1, skip next st] 31 times, *work (dc, ch 1, dc) in next st, ch 1, dc in next st, ch

1, work (dc, ch 1, dc) in next st—corner made, ch 1, skip next st, [dc in next st, ch 1, skip next st] 64 times, repeat from * twice more, work (dc, ch 1, dc) in next st, ch 1, dc in next st, ch 1, work (dc, ch 1, dc) in next st, ch 1, skip next st, [dc in next st, ch 1, skip next st] 32 times, dc in last st—271 ch–1 sps. Turn.
Row 3 Ch 3, dc in first st, dc in next ch–1 sp, [dc in next st, dc in next ch–1 sp] 32 times, *[dc in next ch–1 sp] twice, work 2 dc in next dc, [dc in next ch–1 sp] 3 times, [dc in next st, dc in next ch–1 sp] 64 times; repeat from * twice more, [dc in next ch–1 sp] twice, work 2 dc in next dc, [dc in next ch–1 sp] 3 times, [dc in next st, dc in next ch–1 sp] 31 times, dc in top of ch–3 turning ch—541 sts. Fasten off. Turn.
Row 4 (WS) Join CC with a sl st in first st, ch 1, sc in same st, *ch 4, skip next 4 sts, CL in next st, sc in next st; repeat from * to across—90 CL. Fasten off.

Finishing
Sew short side edges of lace trim together. Weave in all loose ends. Place napkin wrong side up on work surface. With wrong side of lace trim facing up and working through bottom loops of beg chain, pin inner corners of lace trim to outer corners of napkin. Continue to pin bottom loops of beg chain to edge of napkin all around. Working from wrong side, whipstitch bottom loops to edge of napkin using sewing needle and one strand of sewing thread.

How To
Whipstitch bottom loops of trim to edge of napkin. (Shown here in contrasting thread; use matching thread for best results.)

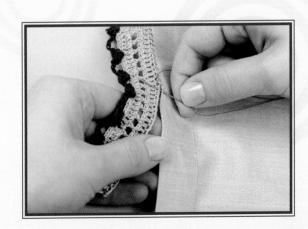

Intricate lace leaves form a crochet border on linen fabric in this stunning piece. It makes a beautiful accessory at Thanksgiving, or any time of the year.

Stitch Glossary

tr2tog (tr 2 stitches together) *Yo twice, insert hook in next indicated st, yo and draw up a lp, [yo and draw through 2 lps on hook] twice; repeat from * once more, yo and draw through all 3 lps on hook.

tr3tog (treble crochet 3 stitches together) *Yo twice, insert hook in next indicated st, yo and draw up a lp, [yo and draw through 2 lps on hook] twice; repeat from * 2 more times, yo and draw through all 4 lps on hook.

Finished Measurements

Approx 22"/56cm wide x 47"/119.5cm long (5"/12.5cm wide edging; 12 x 37"/30.5 x 94cm fabric center).

Gauge

39 sts and 18 rows = 4"/10cm over double crochet.
Remember to check gauge for best results!

How To Make a Gauge Swatch
Ch 41.
Row 1 Dc in 4th ch from hook (beg ch counts as first dc), dc in each remaining ch across—39 dc.
Rows 2–18 Ch 3 (counts as first dc here and throughout), turn, dc in each st across.

Yarn

AUNT LYDIA'S *Classic Crochet Thread*, Size 10, each ball approx 400yd/365m (cotton)
• 2 balls #226 Natural

Crochet Hooks

Size 7 (1.65mm) steel crochet hook *or size to obtain gauge*

Additional

13½" x 38½"/34cm x 98cm piece of Newcastle Linen, 40 ct; zweigart.com
Sewing needle or sewing machine
Matching sewing thread
Pins
Stitch markers
Yarn needle

Resulting gauge swatch should measure approx. 4 x 4"/10 x10cm. Adjust hook size if necessary to obtain correct gauge.

Notes

1 Place a stitch marker in every 50th ch of foundation ch, to make counting chs easier.
2 On Round 1, place a st marker in every 50th dc on each side between the 5–dc corners, to make counting sts on each side easier.
3 In Rounds 2 through 13, place a st marker in each corner ch–sp to identify the corners on the next round.

Edging

Ch 944; taking care not to twist ch, join with sl st in first ch to form a ring.
Round 1 (RS) Ch 3 (counts as first dc here and throughout), dc in next 114 ch, *5 dc in next ch (corner made), dc in next 355 ch, 5 dc in next ch (corner made)*; dc in next 115 ch; repeat from * to * once; join with sl st in top of beg ch—960 dc.
Note After completing round 1, lay piece on a flat surface to ensure that it is not twisted. Piece may tend to curl, but will flatten out as more rounds are worked.
Round 2 Sl st in next 3 dc, ch 8, sk next 5 dc, dc in next dc, ch 5, sk next 5 dc, dc in next dc; *ch 3, sk next 5 dc, (tr, ch 3, tr) in next dc, ch 3, sk next 5 dc, dc in next dc, [ch 5, sk next 5 dc, dc in next dc] 2 times; repeat from * across to 3 sts before next 5–dc corner; ch 5, sk next 5 dc, (tr, ch 5, tr) in next dc (center dc of 5–dc corner) (corner ch–sp made)**; [ch 5, sk next 5 dc, dc in next dc] 3 times; repeat from * 3 more times, ending last repeat at **; ch 5; join with sl st in 3rd ch of beg ch—4 corner (tr, ch 5, tr), 4 (tr, ch 3, tr) on each short side and 14 (tr, ch 3, tr) on each long side.

Round 3 Sl st in next 3 ch, ch 8, dc in 3rd ch of next ch–5 sp; *ch 4, sk next dc, 3 tr in next tr, ch 5, 3 tr in next tr, ch 4, sk next dc, dc in 3rd ch of next ch–5 sp, ch 5, dc in 3rd ch of next ch–5 sp; repeat from * across to next corner; ch 5, sk next dc, 3 tr in next tr, ch 3, (tr, ch 5, tr) in 3rd ch of next ch–5 sp (corner ch–sp made), ch 3, 3 tr in next tr, ch 5, sk next dc**; dc in 3rd ch of next ch–5 sp, ch 5, dc in 3rd ch of next ch–5 sp; repeat from * 3 more times, ending last repeat at **; join with sl st in 3rd ch of beg ch.
Round 4 Sl st in next 3 ch, ch 7; *sk next dc, 2 tr in next 3 tr, ch 2, dc in 3rd ch of next ch–5 sp, ch 2, 2 tr in next 3 tr, ch 4, sk next dc, dc in 3rd ch of next ch–5 sp, ch 4; repeat from * across to next corner; dc in 3rd ch of next ch–5 sp, ch 2, 2 tr in next 3 tr, ch 5, sk next tr, (tr, ch 5, tr) in 3rd ch of next ch–5 sp (corner ch–sp made), ch 5, sk next tr, 2 tr in next 3 tr, ch 2**; [dc in 3rd ch of next ch–5 sp, ch 4] 2 times; repeat from * 3 more times, ending last repeat at **; dc in 3rd ch of next ch–5 sp, ch 4; join with sl st in 3rd ch of beg ch.
Round 5 Sl st in next 2 ch, ch 6; *[tr2tog over next 2 tr] 3 times, ch 3, 3 tr in next dc, ch 3, [tr2tog over next 2 tr] 3 times, ch 3, dc in 3rd ch of next ch–4 sp, ch 3, dc in 2nd ch of next ch–4 sp**; ch 3; repeat from * across to next corner, ending last repeat at **; ch 5, [tr2tog over next 2 tr] 3 times, ch 5, 3 tr in next tr, ch 3, (tr, ch 5, tr) in 3rd ch of next ch–5 sp (corner ch–sp made), ch 3, 3 tr in next tr, ch 5, [tr2tog over next 2 tr] 3 times, ch 5, sk next dc, dc in 3rd ch of next ch–4 sp, ch 3***; dc in 2nd ch of next ch–4 sp, ch 3; repeat from * 3 more times, ending last repeat at ***; join with sl st in 3rd ch of beg ch.
Round 6 Sl st in next 3 ch and in next tr2tog, ch 3, tr2tog over next 2 tr2tog; *ch 4, 2 tr in next 3 tr, ch 4, tr3tog over next 3 tr2tog, ch 4, sk next ch–3 sp**; tr in 2nd ch of next ch–3 sp, ch 4, tr3tog over next 3 tr2tog; repeat from * across to next corner, ending last repeat at **; (tr, ch 5, tr) in 2nd ch of next ch–3 sp, ch 4, tr3tog over next 3 tr2tog, ch 5, 2 tr in next 3 tr, ch 5, sk next ch–3 sp, (tr, ch 5, tr) in 3rd ch of next ch–5 sp (corner ch–sp made), ch 5, sk next ch–3 sp, 2 tr in next 3 tr, ch 5, tr3tog over next 3 tr2tog, ch 4, sk next ch–5 sp, (tr, ch 5, tr) in 2nd ch of next ch–3 sp, ch 4***; tr3tog over next 3 tr2tog; repeat from * 3 more times, ending last repeat at ***; join with sl st in first tr2tog.
Round 7 Sl st in next 2 ch, ch 7; *[tr2tog over next 2 tr] 3 times, ch 4, dc in 3rd ch of next ch–4 sp**; ch 4, sk next ch–4 sp, (tr, ch 3, tr) in next tr, ch 4, sk next ch–4 sp, dc in 2nd ch of next ch–4 sp, ch 4; repeat from * across to next corner, ending last repeat at **; ***ch 3, dc in 2nd ch of

next ch–4 sp, ch 3, (tr, ch 3, tr) in 3rd ch of next ch–5 sp, ch 3, dc in 3rd ch of next ch–4 sp, ch 3***; dc in 3rd ch of next ch–5 sp, ch 5, [tr2tog over next 2 tr] 3 times, ch 5, 3 tr in next tr, ch 3, (tr, ch 5, tr) in 3rd ch of next ch–5 sp (corner ch–sp made), ch 3, 3 tr in next tr, ch 5, [tr2tog over next 2 tr] 3 times, ch 5, dc in 3rd ch of next ch–5 sp; repeat from *** to *** once; dc in 2nd ch of next ch–4 sp, ch 4; repeat from * 3 more times, omitting last dc and ch–4 on last repeat; join with sl st in 3rd ch of beg ch.

Round 8 Sl st in next 4 ch and in next tr2tog, ch 3, tr2tog over next 2 tr2tog; *ch 4, dc in 3rd ch of next ch–4 sp, ch 3, sk next ch–4 sp, 3 tr in next tr, ch 5, 3 tr in next tr, ch 3, sk next ch–4 sp, dc in 2nd ch of next ch–4 sp, ch 4, tr3tog over next 3 tr2tog; repeat from * across to next corner; ch 4, tr2tog over 3rd ch of next ch–4 sp and 2nd ch of next ch–3 sp, ch 4, sk next ch–3 sp, 3 tr in next tr, ch 5, 3 tr in next tr, ch 4, sk next ch–3 sp, tr2tog over 2nd ch of next ch–3 sp and 3rd ch of next ch–5 sp, ch 5, tr3tog over next 3 tr2tog, ch 5, 2 tr in next 3 tr, ch 5, sk next ch–3 sp, (tr, ch 5, tr) in 3rd ch of next ch–5 sp (corner ch–sp made), ch 5, sk next ch–3 sp, 2 tr in next 3 tr, ch 5, tr3tog over next 3 tr2tog, ch 5, tr2tog over 3rd ch of next ch–5 sp and 2nd ch of next ch–3 sp, ch 4, sk next ch–3 sp, 3 tr in next tr, ch 5, 3 tr in next tr, ch 4, sk next ch–3 sp, tr2tog over 2nd ch of next ch–3 sp and 2nd ch of next ch–4 sp, ch 4, tr3tog over next 3 tr2tog; repeat from * 3 more times, omitting last tr3tog on last repeat; join with sl st in next tr2tog.

Round 9 Ch 7, sk next 2 ch–sps; *2 tr in next 3 tr, ch 2, dc in 3rd ch of next ch–5 sp, ch 2, 2 tr in next 3 tr, ch 4**; sk next 2 ch–sps***; dc in next tr3tog, ch 4, sk

next 2 ch–sps; repeat from * across to next corner, ending last repeat at **; sk next ch–4 sp, [dc in 3rd ch of next ch–5 sp, ch 4] 2 times, [tr2tog over next 2 tr] 3 times, ch 5, 3 tr in next tr, ch 3, (tr, ch 5, tr) in 3rd ch of next ch–5 sp (corner ch–sp made), ch 3, 3 tr in next tr, ch 5, [tr2tog over next 2 tr] 3 times, ch 4, [dc in 3rd ch of next ch–5 sp, ch 4] 2 times, sk next ch–4 sp; repeat from * 3 more times; repeat from * to *** once; join with sl st in 3rd ch of beg ch.

Round 10 Sl st in next 2 ch, ch 6; *[tr2tog over next 2 tr] 3 times; ch 3, 3 tr in next dc, ch 3, [tr2tog over next 2 tr] 3 times**; ch 3, dc in 3rd ch of next ch–4 sp, ch 3***; dc in 2nd ch of next ch–4 sp, ch 3; repeat from * across to next corner, ending last repeat at **; ch 4, [dc in 3rd ch of next ch–4 sp, ch 3] 3 times, tr3tog over next 3 tr2tog, ch 5, 2 tr in next 3 tr, ch 5, sk next ch–3 sp, (tr, ch 5, tr) in 3rd ch of next ch–5 sp (corner ch–sp made), ch

5, sk next ch–3 sp, 2 tr in next 3 tr, ch 5, tr3tog over next 3 tr2tog, [ch 3, dc in 2nd ch of next ch–4 sp] 3 times; ch 4; repeat from * 3 more times; repeat from * to *** once; join with sl st in 3rd ch of beg ch.

Round 11 Sl st in next 3 ch and in next tr2tog, ch 3, tr2tog over next 2 tr2tog; *ch 4, 2 tr in next 3 tr, ch 4, tr3tog over next 3 tr2tog, ch 4**; sk next ch–3 sp, tr in 2nd ch of next ch–3 sp, ch 4***; sk next ch–3 sp, tr3tog over next 3 tr2tog; repeat from * across to next corner, ending last repeat at **; sk next ch–4 sp, (tr, ch 5, tr) in 2nd ch of next ch–3 sp, ch 4, sk next ch–3 sp, dc in 2nd ch of next ch–3 sp, ch 4, dc in 3rd ch of next ch–5 sp, ch 4, [tr2tog over next 2 tr] 3 times, ch 5, tr in next tr, ch 3, (tr, ch 5, tr) in 3rd ch of next ch–5 sp (corner ch–sp made), ch 3, tr in next tr, ch 5, [tr2tog over next 2 tr] 3 times, ch 4, dc in 3rd ch of next ch–5 sp, ch 4, dc in 2nd ch of next ch–3 sp, ch 4, sk next ch–3 sp, (tr, ch 5, tr) in 2nd ch of next ch–3 sp, ch 4, sk next ch–4 sp, tr3tog over next 3 tr2tog; repeat from * 3 more times; repeat from * to *** once; join with sl st in first tr2tog.

Round 12 Sl st in next 2 ch, ch 7; *[tr2tog over next 2 tr] 3 times, ch 4, dc in 3rd ch of next ch–4 sp**; ch 4, sk next ch–4 sp, (tr, ch 3, tr) in next tr, ch 4****; sk next ch–4 sp, dc in 2nd ch of next ch–4 sp, ch 4; repeat from * across to next corner, ending last repeat at **; ***ch 3, dc in 2nd ch of next ch–4 sp, ch 4, sc in 3rd ch of next ch–5 sp, ch 4, dc in 3rd ch of next ch–4 sp, ch 3***; [dc in 2nd ch of next ch–4 sp, ch 4] 2 times, tr3tog over next 3 tr2tog, ch 4, dc in 3rd ch of next ch–5 sp, ch 5, sk next tr, tr in next tr, ch 3, (tr, ch 5, tr) in 3rd ch of next ch–5 sp (corner ch–sp made), ch 3, tr in next tr, ch 5, sk next tr, dc in 3rd ch of next ch–5 sp,

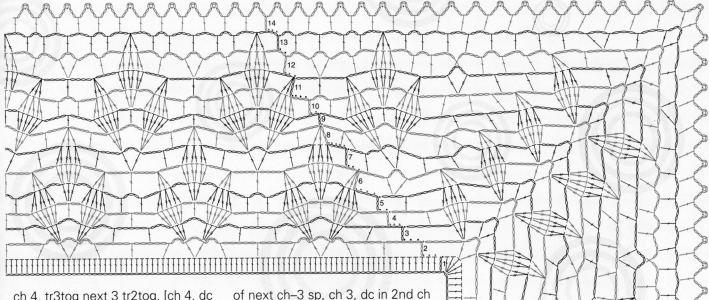

ch 4, tr3tog next 3 tr2tog, [ch 4, dc in 3rd ch of next ch–4 sp] 2 times; repeat from *** to *** once; dc in 2nd ch of next ch–4 sp, ch 4; repeat from * 3 more times; repeat from * to **** once; join with sl st in 3rd ch of beg ch.

Round 13 Sl st in next 2 ch, ch 7; *tr3tog over next 3 tr2tog; **ch 4, dc in 3rd ch of next ch–sp, ch 3, dc in 2nd ch of next ch–sp, ch 4**; dc in 2nd ch of next ch–3 sp***; repeat from ** to ** once; repeat from * across to next corner; tr3tog over next 3 tr2tog, [ch 4, dc in 3rd ch of next ch–sp, ch 3, dc in 2nd ch of next ch–sp] 2 times, ch 4, dc in 2nd ch of next ch–sp, [ch 4, dc in 3rd ch of next ch–sp] 2 times, ch 3, dc in 2nd ch of next ch–sp, ch 3, (dc, ch 3, dc) in 3rd ch of next ch–5 sp, ch 3, dc in 2nd ch of next ch–3 sp, ch 3, (tr, ch 5, tr) in 3rd ch of next ch–5 sp (corner ch–sp made), ch 3, dc in 2nd ch of next ch–3 sp, ch 3, (dc, ch 3, dc) in 3rd ch of next ch–5 sp, ch 3, dc in 3rd ch of next ch–sp, ch 3, [dc in 2nd ch of next ch–sp, ch 4] 3 times, dc in 3rd ch of next ch–sp, ch 3, dc in 2nd ch of next ch–sp, ch 4, dc in 2nd ch

of next ch–3 sp, ch 3, dc in 2nd ch of next ch–4 sp, ch 4; repeat from * 3 more times; repeat from * to *** once; ch 4, dc in 3rd ch of next ch–sp, ch 3; join with sl st in 3rd ch of beg ch.

Round 14 Sl st in next 2 ch and in ch–sp, ch 8, sl st in 3rd ch from hook, ch 2; *dc in next ch–sp, ch 5, sl st in 3rd ch from hook, ch 2**; repeat from * across to next corner; [dc, ch 5, sl st in 3rd ch from hook, ch 2, dc] in corner ch–sp, ch 5, sl st in 3rd ch from hook, ch 2; repeat from * 3 more times; repeat from * to ** across to beg ch; join with sl st in 3rd ch of beg ch. Fasten off.

Finishing
Weave in all ends. Wash and block edging to inner dimensions of 12 x 37"/30.5 x 94cm and outer dimensions of 22 x 47"/56 x 119.5cm.

Hemming Linen Fabric
Fold one edge of linen ¼"/0.5cm twice to wrong side. Iron folded edge, if desired. Repeat folding on other 3 edges of linen. Pin in place. With thread and sewing machine or sewing needle, sew close to inside

fold through all 3 layers for hem.

Assembly
With right sides of edging and linen facing, pin edging to hemmed edges of linen with inner edge of edging along sewn hemline and top of round 1 sts at edges of linen. With thread and sewing needle or sewing machine, sew edging to edges of linen.

Tip
When putting work down for a length of time, insert a stitch marker in the last loop to keep stitches from being pulled out.

Yarn

AUNT LYDIA'S *Classic Crochet Thread,*
Size 10, each ball approx 350yd/320m
(mercerized cotton)
- 1 ball #486 Navy (A)
- 1 ball #423 Maize (B)
- 1 ball #397 Wasabi (C)

Crochet Hooks

Size 8 (1.5mm) steel crochet hook *or*
size to obtain gauge

Additional

18 small Susan Bates Luxite rings
1"/25.5mm diameter
16 medium Susan Bates Luxite rings
1½"/38mm diameter
2 large Susan Bates Luxite rings
2"/51mm diameter
Tapestry needle

Snazz up your table with these graphic coasters. They're a cinch to make—just single crochet over plastic rings for a look that's both retro cool and contemporary chic.

Finished Measurements

Approx 4½"/11.5cm wide x 4½"/11.5cm long.

Gauge

Gauge is not essential for this project!

Note

1 Rings are first covered with single crochet stitches. The rings are then arranged and sewn together to make coasters.

2 Use tails to sew rings together wherever possible, or use a single strand of sewing thread matching the darker color.

Covering Rings

Join thread with sl st over ring leaving a 4"/10cm tail. The side facing you is now the right side of the ring.

Round 1 Making sure to work tightly and evenly so that there is no space between the sts and the sts do not overlap, repeatedly sc over the ring until about ¼"/6mm of the ring remains uncovered; working over tail, work more sc over the ring and tail; join with sl st in first sc. Fasten off leaving a 6"/15cm tail for sewing. Pull on 4"/10cm tail to remove slack; cut off tail close to sts.

Coaster 1

Cover four small rings with A, one small ring with B, and four medium rings with C. Arrange rings as shown in photo, with right sides facing up. Sew large C rings to small B ring. Sew small A rings to large C rings.

Coaster 2

Cover four small rings with A, one small ring with C, and four medium rings with B. Arrange and sew rings as for Coaster 1.

Coaster 3

Cover four small rings with C, four medium rings with A, and one large ring with B. Arrange rings as shown in photo, with right sides facing up. Sew medium A rings to large B ring. Sew small C rings between the medium A rings.

Coaster 4

Cover four small rings with B, four medium rings with A, and one large ring with C. Arrange and sew rings as for Coaster 3.

Weave in all ends.

Tip

You can use this technique to make placemats or a table runner—just cover extra rings and sew them together as described in the pattern.

Rose Callahan

Stitch these in any combo of four complementary hues. Make the small, inside square alone to use as a coaster.

Stitch Glossary

CL (cluster) [Yarn over, insert hook in st or sp indicated, yarn over and draw up a loop, yarn over and draw through 2 loops on hook] 3 times, yarn over and draw through all 4 loops on hook.

shell Work 5 dc in st or sp indicated.
scallop Work (sc, hdc, 5 dc, hdc, sc) in sp indicated.
large shell ([tr, ch 1] 4 times, tr) in st indicated.
picot Ch 3, sl st in sc before ch–3.

Finished Measurements
Approx 12¾"/32cm square

Gauge
Rounds 1–3 = 2"/5cm square
Remember to check gauge for best results!

Placemat

With A, ch 5; join with sl st in first ch to form a ring.
Round 1 (RS) Ch 3 (counts as first dc now and throughout), 2 dc in ring, [ch 3, 3 dc in ring] 3 times, ch 3; join with sl st in 3rd ch of beg ch–3—4 groups of 3 dc and 4 corner ch–3 sps.
Round 2 Working in back loop of each dc and ch around, ch 3, dc in next 2 dc; *dc in next ch, ch 3, sk next ch, dc in next ch**; dc in next 3 dc; repeat

Yarn

AUNT LYDIA'S *Fashion Crochet Thread*, size 3, each ball approx 150yd/137m (cotton)

2 balls each (makes 4 placemats):
- #264 Lime (A)
- #65 Warm Teal (B)
- #625 Sage (C)
- #486 Navy (D)

Crochet Hooks

Size 2 (2.25mm) steel crochet hook *or size to obtain gauge*

Additional

Yarn needle

from * around, ending last repeat at **; join—4 groups of 5 dc and 4 corner ch–3 sps.

Round 3 Working in back loop of each dc and ch around, ch 3, dc in next 3 dc; *dc in next ch, ch 5, sk next ch, dc in next ch**; dc in next 5 dc; repeat from * around, ending last repeat at **; dc in next dc; join—4 groups of 7 dc and 4 corner ch–5 sps. Fasten off.

Round 4 With right side facing, join B with sl st in first dc of any 7–dc group; working in back loop of each dc and ch around, ch 3, dc in next 6 dc; *dc in next ch, ch 3, sk next ch, CL in next ch, ch 3, sk next ch, dc in next ch**; dc in next 7 dc; repeat from * around, ending last repeat at **; join—4 CL, 4 groups of 9 dc and 8 ch–3 sps.

Round 5 Working in back loop of each dc and ch around, ch 3, dc in next dc; *ch 1, sk next dc, CL in next dc, ch 1, sk next dc, dc in next 3 dc, dc in next ch, ch 3, sk next ch, CL in next ch, ch 3, sk next CL, CL in next ch, ch 3, sk next ch, dc in next ch**; dc in next 3 dc; repeat from * around, ending last repeat at **; dc in next dc; join—12 CL, 8 groups of 4 dc, 12 ch–3 sps and 8 ch–1 sps.

Round 6 Working in back loop of each dc and ch around, ch 3, dc in next dc; *ch 3, sk next ch, sk next CL, sk next ch, dc in next 4 dc, dc in next ch, ch 5, sk next 2 chs, sk next CL, sk next ch, shell in next ch, ch 5, sk next ch, sk next CL, sk next 2 chs, dc in next ch**; dc in next 4 dc; repeat from * around, ending last repeat at **; dc in next 2 dc; join—4 shells, 8 groups of 5 dc, 8 ch–5 sps and 4 ch–3 sps. Fasten off.

Round 7 With right side facing, join C with sl st in first dc of first 5–dc group after any shell, working in back loop of each dc and ch around, ch 3, dc in each dc and ch around, working (dc, ch 3, dc) in center dc of each shell; join—4 corner ch–3 sps and 29 dc on each side. Fasten off.

Round 8 With right side facing, join D with sc in any corner ch–3 sp, ch 3, sc in same sp as joining; *[ch 3, sk next 2 dc, sc in next dc] 9 times; ch 3, sk next 2 dc**; (sc, ch 3, sc) in next corner ch–3 sp; repeat from * around, ending last repeat at **; join with sl st in first sc—4 corner ch–3 sps and 10 ch–3 sps on each side.

Round 9 Sl st in corner ch–3 sp, ch 3, (dc, ch 3, 2 dc) in same ch–3 sp; *ch 2, CL in next ch–3 sp; repeat from * across to next corner ch–3 sp; ch 2**; (2 dc, ch 3, 2 dc) in next corner ch–3 sp; repeat from * around, ending last repeat at **; join with sl st in 3rd ch of beg ch–3—4 corner ch–3 sps, 16 dc and 10 CL on each side. Fasten off.

Round 10 With right side facing, join C with sl st in any corner ch–3 sp, ch 3, (dc, ch 3, 2 dc) in same sp as joining; *ch 2, sk next 2 dc, 2 dc in next ch–2 sp, [dc in next CL, 2 dc in next ch–2 sp] 10 times, ch 2, sk next 2 dc**; (2 dc, ch 3, 2 dc) in next corner ch–3 sp; repeat from * around, ending last repeat at **; join—4 corner ch–3 sps, 8 ch–2 sps and 36 dc on each side. Fasten off.

Round 11 With right side facing, join D with sc in any corner ch–3 sp, ch 3, sc in same sp as joining; *ch 3, sk next 2 dc, sc in next ch–2 sp, [ch 3, sk next 2 dc, sc in next dc] 10 times, ch 3, sk next 2 dc, sc in next ch–2 sp, ch 3, sk next 2 dc**; (sc, ch 3, sc) in next corner ch–3 sp; repeat from * around, ending last repeat at **; join with sl st in first sc—4 corner ch–3 sps and 13 ch–3 sps on each side.

Round 12 Repeat Round 9—4 corner ch–3 sps, 16 dc and 13 CL on each side. Fasten off.

Round 13 With right side facing, join A with sl st in any corner ch–3 sp, ch 3, (dc, ch 5, 2 dc) in same sp as joining; *ch 2, sk next 2 dc, 2 dc in next ch–2 sp, [dc in next CL, 2 dc in next ch–2 sp] 13 times, ch 2, sk next 2 dc**; (2 dc, ch 5, 2 dc) in next corner ch–3 sp; repeat from * around, ending last repeat at **; join—4 corner ch–5 sps, 8 ch–2 sps and 45 dc on each side.

Round 14 Ch 1, sc in same ch as joining; *ch 3, (3 dc, ch 4, 3 dc) in next corner ch–5 sp, ch 3, sk next dc, sc in next dc, ch 3, sc in next dc, [ch 7, sk next 6 dc, sc in next dc, ch 3, sk next 3 dc, sc in next dc] 3 times, ch 7, sk next 6 dc, sc in next dc**; ch 3, sc in next dc; repeat from * around, ending last repeat at **; ch 1, join with hdc in first sc (counts as ch–3 sp)—4 corner ch–4 sps, 24 dc, 7 ch–3 sps on each side and 4 ch–7 sps on each side.

Round 15 Ch 1, sc around post of hdc; *ch 3, dc in next 3 dc, (3 dc, ch 4, 3 dc) in next corner ch–4 sp, dc in next 3 dc, ch 3, sk next ch–3 sp, [sc in next ch–3 sp, ch 2, work scallop in next ch–7 sp, ch 2] 4 times**; sc in next ch–3 sp; repeat from * around, ending last repeat at **; join with sl st in first sc—4 corner ch–4 sps, 4 scallops on each side and 12 dc on each side. Fasten off.

Round 16 With right side facing, join B with sl st in any corner ch–4 sp, ch 3, (2 dc, ch 4, 3 dc) in same sp as joining; *dc in next 3 dc, ch 3, sk next 2 dc, sc in next dc, [ch 2, large shell in next sc, ch 2, sc in 3rd dc of next scallop] 4 times, ch 2, large shell in next sc, ch 2, sc in next dc, ch 3, sk next 2 dc, dc in next 3 dc**; (3 dc, ch 4, 3 dc)

pepped-up Placemats

in next corner ch–4 sp; repeat from * around, ending last repeat at **; join with sl st in 3rd ch of beg ch–3—4 corner ch–4 sps, 5 large shells on each side and 12 dc on each side.

Round 17 Ch 3, dc in next 2 dc; *(2 dc, ch 5, 2 dc) in next corner ch–4 sp, dc in next 6 dc, ch 2, sk next sc, dc in next tr, ch 2, sk next tr, sc in next tr, ch 2, sk next tr, dc in next tr, [ch 2, dc in next sc, ch 2, dc in next tr, ch 2, sk next tr, sc in next tr, ch 2, sk next tr, dc in next tr] 4 times, ch 2, sk next sc**; dc in next 6 dc; repeat from * around, ending last repeat at **; dc in next 3 dc; join—4 corner ch–5 sps and 20 ch–2 sps on each side. Fasten off.

Round 18 With right side facing, join C with sl st in any corner ch–5 sp, ch 3, (2 dc, ch 4, 3 dc) in same sp as joining;

*dc in next 8 dc, [2 dc in next ch–2 sp, dc in next st] 20 times, dc in next 7 dc**; (3 dc, ch 4, 3 dc) in next corner ch–5 sp; repeat from * around, ending last repeat at **; join—4 corner ch–4 sps and 81 dc on each side. Fasten off.

Round 19 With right side facing, join D with sc in any corner ch–4 sp, ch 4, sc in same sp as joining; *ch 3, sk next 2 dc, sc in next dc, [ch 3, sk next 3 dc, sc in next dc] 19 times; ch 3, sk next 2 dc**; (sc, ch 4, sc) in next corner ch–4 sp; repeat from * around, ending last repeat at **; join with sl st in first sc—4 corner ch–4 sps and 21 ch–3 sps on each side.

Round 20 Sl st in next corner ch–4 sp, ch 3, (2 dc, ch 3, 3 dc) in same ch–4 sp; *[ch 3, CL in next ch–3 sp] 21

times, ch 3**; (3 dc, ch 3, 3 dc) in next corner ch–4 sp; repeat from * around, ending last repeat at **; join with sl st in 3rd ch of beg ch–3—4 corner ch–3 sps, 24 dc and 21 CL on each side.

Round 21 Ch 1, sc in same ch as joining, sc in next 2 dc; *(2 sc, picot, 2 sc) in next corner ch–4 sp, sc in next 3 dc, [(3 sc, picot) in next ch–3 sp, ch 1, sk next CL] 21 times, 3 sc in next ch–3 sp**; sc in next 3 dc; repeat from * around, ending last repeat at **; join with sl st in first sc—4 corner picots and 21 picots on each side. Fasten off.

Finishing
Weave in all ends.